I Brought the War with Me

I Brought the War with Me

Stories and Poems from the Front Line

LINDSEY HILSUM

Chatto & Windus

LONDON

1 3 5 7 9 10 8 6 4 2

Chatto & Windus, an imprint of Vintage, is part of the Penguin Random House group
of companies whose addresses can be found at global.penguinrandomhouse.com

First published in the UK by Chatto & Windus in 2024

Copyright © Lindsey Hilsum 2024

Lindsey Hilsum has asserted her right to be identified as the author of this
Work in accordance with the Copyright, Designs and Patents Act 1988

penguin.co.uk/vintage

Typeset in 10.8 /14.8 pt Calluna by Jouve (UK), Milton Keynes
Printed and bound in Great Britain by Clays Ltd, Elcograf S.p.A.

The authorised representative in the EEA is Penguin Random House Ireland,
Morrison Chambers, 32 Nassau Street, Dublin D02 YH68

A CIP catalogue record for this book is available from the British Library

ISBN 9781784745349

I brought the war with me
unknowingly, perhaps on my skin, plumes
of it in my hair, under my nails.

Warsan Shire, War Poem

For T. L.

Contents

LOVE

HISTORY

COURAGE

PRISON

CHILDREN

MEMORY

Foreword

In September 2022, a few days after Russian forces retreated from the Ukrainian town of Izium, I was standing outside an apartment block that had been split apart by a missile. Fifty-four residents had been killed in the Russian attack, which had taken place six months earlier. Purple and yellow wild flowers were growing in the rubble that filled the chasm between the two parts of the block.

'It is not the houses. It is the space between the houses,' I thought. 'It is not the streets that exist. It is the streets that no longer exist.' The words of James Fenton's 1981 poem 'A German Requiem', about selective memory in the Second World War, came to me when I could no longer find my own.

Back at my hotel in Kharkiv, I looked it up.

It is not your memories which haunt you.
It is not what you have written down.
It is what you have forgotten, what you must forget.
What you must go on forgetting all your life.

The idea that the spaces between the houses symbolised gaps in memory, and that forgetting might be essential if people were to live together in peace, encapsulated the future facing the Ukrainians I had met that day. After the attack on the apartment block, the Russians had driven out the Ukrainian army, and Izium endured six terrible, violent months of Russian occupation. A young couple told me that now the Ukrainian authorities were back, they planned to denounce their neighbours for collaboration with the occupiers. I couldn't know if the neighbours really had collaborated with the Russians, or just done what they deemed necessary to survive. Either way, war had brought bitterness and enmity in its wake. Just like those in Fenton's poem, from now on people's lives in Izium would be polluted by suspicion, by the mistrustful look and the whispered word behind the hand.

It is not what he wants to know.
It is what he wants not to know.
It is not what they say.
It is what they do not say.

My TV news report reflected some of this, but it did not have the allusive power of the poem.

In my nearly four decades as a foreign correspondent, I have always carried a book of poetry with me. While the images we show have great impact, I feel that journalistic language sometimes fails to convey the intensity of the experience. Maybe James Fenton's poetry resonates with me because he was a war correspondent as well as a poet – he sees what I see but has found a more compelling way of expressing it, as if he is working in three dimensions while I am stuck in two. We journalists pride ourselves on the clarity of our prose and on making complex stories simple. That's our job – to explain why terrible things are happening and to challenge the euphemisms used by politicians and military spokespeople. We also try to convey the thoughts and feelings of the people we meet, and a sense of what it feels like to be on the ground. Yet we may lose the deeper meaning, the universal import of what we have witnessed or the contradictory emotions that war engenders.

Sometimes poetry can serve as a vaccination against despair. On 7th October 2023, militants from the Palestinian group Hamas breached the high-tech fence separating Gaza from Israel and went on a rampage of killing, rape and abduction. It was the single worst massacre of Jews since the Holocaust. Israel proceeded to bomb Gaza relentlessly, destroying homes, killing tens of thousands of civilians and depriving all Gazans of food, water and other basic necessities. The Israel Defense Forces invaded in tanks and armoured vehicles, fighting Hamas which operated out of tunnels. The Israeli government told Gazans to flee to the south of the strip which would be safe. It wasn't – people were killed when bombs hit their tented camps. Many families were forced to flee multiple times – nowhere was safe. Even the dead could not rest in peace, as tanks ploughed up graveyards. Day after day Gazan journalists filmed terrible scenes of injured children, whimpering in overcrowded hospital corridors, sometimes unaware that their parents had been killed. Whatever and however we reported, journalists came under heavy criticism, accused of bias towards one side or the other, depending on the political orientation of the accuser. Stoked by social media, antisemitism and islamophobia surged across the world; everybody, it seemed, wanted to pick a side and deny the humanity of the other, to demand a monopoly on suffering. Slogans and propaganda are an anathema to good journalism as they are to good poetry.

I turned to the most famous Palestinian poet, Mahmoud Darwish, whose work expresses the anger and yearning of those living under occupation and bombardment, who gain strength from their ancestors' long history. 'I have lived on the land long before swords turned man into prey,' he wrote in his poem 'I Belong There'. Then I sought out his Israeli counterpart, Yehuda Amichai, who understood that self-righteous fury rarely leads to peace.

From the place where we are right
Flowers will never grow
In the spring.

The place where we are right
Is hard and trampled
Like a yard.

Poets don't have the answers. But they may help us understand our own actions and reactions and find a way through the darkness.

The lives of those who have had war visited upon them, including children, conscripts and civilians, are desperate and miserable, as the stories in this book make clear. But those who have chosen to visit war – aid workers, journalists, military volunteers – share a secret. War gives your life purpose and meaning. Suddenly you believe you know what matters and what can be dismissed as unimportant. The colours are brighter and the mountains clearer. You live in the moment. There's a wonderful camaraderie with others going through the same experience, and surviving a near miss gives you a heady rush of adrenaline. Shared fear turns to laughter, which no one outside the group can understand. When you go home, or the war ends, you have to return to the humdrum reality of paying the bills and arguing about who takes out the rubbish. Even those who protest against war far from the front line may get caught up in the thrill of the cause and miss that feeling of urgency when it falls away.

As a servant suggests in Shakespeare's *Coriolanus*, not everyone hates war:

Let me have a war, say I; it exceeds peace as far as day does night; it's spritely, waking, audible, and full of vent. Peace is a very apoplexy, lethargy; mull'd, deaf, sleepy, insensible; a getter of more bastard children than war is a destroyer of men.
(*Coriolanus*, Act IV, Scene V)

I came to war reporting reluctantly, having started my career in the late 1970s as a volunteer aid worker in Central America. If I'm honest, I didn't really know that war was brewing across the region – my concern was social justice, and, at twenty years old, I just wanted to have an adventure and change the world. (I succeeded in the former but not – needless to say – in the latter.) In 1982, I moved to Kenya to work for the UN International Children's Emergency Fund, UNICEF. A few years later, when I realised that – having no expertise in anything practical such as public health or agriculture – I was not much use as an aid worker, I pivoted to journalism, which required only the few skills I had, namely the ability to read, write and ask questions. Remaining in Nairobi, I managed to get freelance work for the BBC and the *Guardian*. Still, I tried to avoid war, thinking, somewhat piously, that I should be covering poverty and development. Reality overcame the illusions I harboured. Nearly every country neighbouring Kenya – Uganda, Sudan, Somalia, Ethiopia – was going through civil war. I couldn't avoid it. And I found that while reporting on people in warzones was at times upsetting and occasionally terrifying, it was also rewarding and exciting. I felt that I was living through history as it happened. Later, I was lucky enough to get a job with Channel 4 News, based in London, and while I have never been exclusively a war correspondent, I have spent a lot of my career reporting conflict.

Covering war can be addictive; a colleague who has since weaned himself off it titled his memoir *War Junkie*. My friend Marie Colvin, the *Sunday Times* correspondent who was killed in Syria in 2012, was another addict. After she was shot crossing a front line in Sri Lanka and lost her sight in one eye, she was diagnosed with post-traumatic stress disorder (PTSD). She received psychiatric treatment, recovered and promptly went back to war. 'Anyway,' she shrugged, 'it's what we do.' In recent years there's been more acknowledgement that PTSD is an occupational hazard for journalists who cover war, especially for prolonged periods. At first the research concentrated on western journalists, but now it's recognised that those who report their own country descending into conflict may be more vulnerable, not least because they have family responsibilities and can't just leave if it gets too dangerous.

Despite all this, many journalists are resilient, and – at least for now – I would count myself as fortunate in this regard. Witnessing the suffering of others, surviving danger and experiencing grief are all profound experiences, to which nightmares, anger, tears and bouts of despondency are all normal, human responses. They are not necessarily signs of a clinical condition. Pain and trauma are not the same. In February 1994, during a hiatus in my journalistic career, I went to work for UNICEF again, this time in Kigali, the capital of Rwanda. It was a time of foreboding and sporadic violence but I had no concept of what was to come: you can't prepare for the unimaginable. Two months to the day after I had arrived, a plane carrying the presidents of Rwanda and neighbouring Burundi was shot out of the sky. Almost immediately, men with machetes and nail-studded clubs were out building roadblocks. It was the start of a genocide, in which some 800,000 ethnic Tutsis were slaughtered by their Hutu neighbours and Hutu militia. In those terrifying first few days I was the only foreign correspondent on the streets of Kigali. The terrible things I saw have stayed with me all my life. In the years that followed, I used to feel that I needed philosophical more than psychological help – after seeing what they are capable of, it is hard to believe that human beings are inherently good. As time went by, I found solace in poetry, which provided both a connection and a way of distancing myself from what I had witnessed. Connection because a poet might express similar emotions to my own, and distance because a poem could transform the singularity of my experience into something universal.

The dominance of the Great War soldier-poets – Wilfred Owen, Rupert Brooke, Siegfried Sassoon, Isaac Rosenberg – in British culture and education may lead to the assumption that war poetry is a male preserve, and that western poets have a monopoly on the form. This is far from the case. The first known war poet was a Sumerian high priestess, Enheduana, who lived in Ur, in what is now southern Iraq, in about 2300 BCE. A new translation of her work has just been published. Contemporary poetry, much of it written by women, reflects the fact that modern conflicts tend to kill more civilians than soldiers. The late Irish musician Frank Harte said, 'Those in power write the history; those who suffer write the songs.' A lot of songs and poems have been written in recent years, including by children like thirteen-year-old Amineh Abou Kerech, whose family fled Syria and ended up in Oxford:

> Can anyone teach me
> how to make a homeland?
> Heartfelt thanks if you can,
> heartiest thanks,
> from the house-sparrows,
> the apple-trees of Syria,
> and yours very sincerely.

Viewers who have watched the wars in Iraq, Afghanistan, Syria, Ukraine and the Middle East unfold on TV have told me they struggle to find the words to express their concern, fear and compassion. As conflicts proliferate, they feel as the great Russian poet Anna Akhmatova did in 1919, contemplating the wreckage left by the Great War and the Russian Revolution:

> Why is this century worse than those that have gone before?
> In a stupor of sorrow and grief

it located the blackest wound
but somehow couldn't heal it.

Already overwhelmed by despair, Akhmatova had yet to face the Second World War and Stalin's persecutions, both of which she survived. Her era was indeed amongst the worst in history. In the second part of the twentieth century, Western Europeans and North Americans grew to believe that peace and prosperity were normal, that war was something that happened to other people elsewhere in the world. Now, many feel a sense of dread. History puts our era in perspective, as well as serving as a warning. Poetry helps us see parallels with the past, and puts up a mirror to our fears.

Back in the 1860s, during the American Civil War, Emily Dickinson wrote that poets can tell the truth in a more subtle, and sometimes more effective, way:

Tell all the truth but tell it slant—
Success in Circuit lies

My aim, then, is to marry reporting with poetry, the 'telling it straight' with the 'telling it slant'. This book comprises fifty stories from conflicts I have covered, each twinned with a poem that elucidates or contrasts with it. Sometimes, the poem comes from the same country as the conflict, but mostly I have looked for poems from elsewhere, to establish both the connection and the universality.

In assembling his perennially popular anthology *Other Men's Flowers*, Field Marshal Lord Wavell, who commanded British forces in the Middle East in the Second World War, used the criteria that he should know each poem by heart – all 256 of them. I cannot claim such feats of memory. I have selected some poems I have known and loved for years, and others that I have only recently discovered. Poetry, like most things, goes in fashions. Lord Wavell favoured iambic pentameter, strict rhyme and a patriotic spirit; I prefer free verse and a more ambiguous and reflective approach. Most of the poems I have chosen are modern, but I have included a few from before the twentieth century. I am drawn to what Wilfred Owen described as: 'The pity of war, the pity war distilled.' Readers will inevitably wish that I had included their favourites, but I have omitted some of my favourites too, because I limited myself to fifty, and I wanted to explore new poetry from the countries where I have travelled.

Inevitably, many of my stories are tragic, but I hope that a few reveal the surreal, absurd and occasionally heartwarming situations that war throws up amidst the fear and sorrow. There is not a lot about weaponry and tactics, and it's not an objective account of the conflicts of the last few decades, but I hope it gives some insight into the way war transforms the lives of those who find themselves caught up in it. Rather than following a chronology, or dividing the book up geographically, I have sorted the stories and poems by theme. Every conflict is different, but the experience of war is in some ways similar, whenever and wherever it happens.

Lindsey Hilsum,
London, June 2024

FIGHTERS

How easy it is to make a ghost

Despite artificial intelligence and autonomous military drones, war is often still fought as it was more than a century ago. The trenches of eastern Ukraine in the winter of 2022 would have been only too familiar to the poets of the First World War who saw combat in the Somme. Of course there are changes – advanced weapons systems, remote targeting, female soldiers – but nonetheless, war frequently comes down to young men risking death to kill other young men, just as it always has done. Some of the soldiers I have met were utterly convinced by the cause for which they risked their lives, while others were plagued by cynicism and doubt. Once you strip away the opposing religious or patriotic convictions, the similarities between enemies can be almost unbearable.

Donbas, Ukraine

November 2022

Autumn was turning to winter in eastern Ukraine, and the trenches were sticky with mud. Water sloshed up to the ankles of our rubber boots as we made our way to the lookout point, where twenty-two-year-old Vadym was peering through binoculars.

'How far away is the enemy?' I asked.

'About five hundred metres,' he replied.

'That's not very far,' I said. The boom of outgoing fire reverberated from another part of the trench complex.

Vadym led me through the labyrinth and down some steps to the surprisingly cosy sleeping quarters that the soldiers had hollowed out. They'd even hung a piece of cloth as a privacy curtain between their bunks and rigged up a rough table for their few comforts: a Snickers bar, a small gas stove, a comb. Vadym's tabby kitten, Olenka, climbed onto his shoulder. She was his companion and his mascot, as well as a good mouser. (Trenches always attract rats and mice.) He had lived in the Netherlands before the war, he said, but had returned to fight the Russians after they invaded in February 2022. His girlfriend was living in the Czech Republic.

I was with a TV team. We made our way back along the trench, bent over so as not to expose ourselves, but the cracks and booms of outgoing fire were growing louder. Suddenly I heard a different and unmistakeable long whistle: a single incoming sniper shot. We slid down the mud sides low into the trench.

Another shot. Then another. The commander moved along silently, straightened up and took aim at the Russian lines. We waited, crouched on our haunches, while the soldiers tried to suppress the sniper. Time passed. Ten minutes? Fifteen? I'm not sure. I wasn't frightened, because as long as we were hunkered down in the trench, I figured we'd probably be safe. But might we have to wait for hours in the cold? We were lucky. After a quiet interlude, we took our chance, dashing across the open ground from one trench to the next and on to safety.

For us it had been a brief moment of jeopardy, but as the wet mud froze, the Ukrainian soldiers would be living in these trenches all through the winter. A hundred years before the Russian invasion of Ukraine, just after the First World War, A. E. Housman captured in thirty-eight words, most of just one syllable, the impulse that drives young men to fight. Vadym had no doubts about the cause for which he was fighting. His country had been invaded, and young men like him had a duty to defend not only Ukraine but also democracy. Anything else would be a source of shame.

Vadym said, 'If we win, my children will live in a free country.'

Here Dead Lie We

A. E. Housman, 1922

Here dead lie we because we did not choose
To live and shame the land from which we sprung.
Life, to be sure, is nothing much to lose;
But young men think it is, and we were young.

Fallujah, Iraq

November 2004

The Americans called the Second Battle of Fallujah Operation Phantom Fury. It was said to be the most intense urban combat the US military had seen since the Battle of Huế in Vietnam in 1968. We were embedded with India Company, 3rd Battalion, 5th Marines, in armoured vehicles.

The euphoria that had greeted the overthrow of the Iraqi dictator, Saddam Hussein, eighteen months earlier had faded. The Americans were now seen not as liberators but as occupiers. Fighters connected to the jihadi group al-Qaeda controlled Fallujah and had been responsible for the killing and mutilation of several American contractors that April. The US military lived behind barbed wire and blast walls. Every time they emerged they risked being blown up either by an improvised explosive device or by unexploded ordnance that littered the area. Every small boy they spotted might be a lookout for the insurgents or sent to lay a trip wire.

I listened to the marines chatting in the armoured vehicle as we approached the staging point and took notes on what they said. It revealed so much more than my interviews.

'I don't like spray and pray. I like to snipe those motherfuckers. Two shots an' he's dead – one in the chest and one in the head,' said one.

'You know what I think of this country? I think, why am I here?' replied his buddy.

7

'You signed up.'

'Yeah. I guess there are some good people but we jus' don't have nothin' to do with 'em.'

'What I hate is that we have to play by the rules and they don't,' another chipped in.

We lived in the armoured vehicle for a week, trying to sleep on planks laid across the bench seats as it reared up, engine roaring, to push down walls twenty-four hours a day. When they weren't fighting or sleeping, the marines sat in the vehicle and watched the scatological cartoon *South Park* on someone's laptop.

Iraqis called Fallujah the City of Mosques. The day of the fiercest battle, India Company was combing a mosque for weapons when it came under AK-47 fire from the surrounding houses. The subsequent battle was intense. I watched from the armoured vehicle as a squad of marines climbed up to a flat roof to provide covering fire for another squad that had been pinned down in a neighbouring building with one man injured. They brought in heavier weapons to suppress incoming fire and enable the rescue of their wounded comrade. A marine pulled the barrel of his M16 to his face and kissed it before firing. The insurgents were still shooting, so the Americans opened up with an anti-tank missile and called in an airstrike. By then I was also on the roof – the explosion was so close it showered us with grit and debris. The sound was deafening, and a massive plume of black smoke rose. Tanks lumbered down the street to turn more firepower on the insurgents. By dusk, no more small arms fire was coming from the neighbourhood. The marines went to check the houses and found the bodies of twenty-one enemy fighters. Three marines from India Company had been killed and twenty-five injured.

For a moment, it was silent. A sickle moon rose over the ruined City of Mosques.

From the marine point of view, it had been a textbook battle – victory by overwhelming force. But for what? Iraq would never come under US control. The day before the battle, the command-ing officer, Major-General Richard Natonski, had given the troops a pep talk. 'Your grandfathers and fathers fought in Vietnam, Korea, World War I and World War II. You are every bit as good as they were,' he said. 'Twenty-five years from now, you're going to be sitting with your grandchild on your lap, and he'll ask you what you did in the war, and you're going to say: I fought in Fallujah.'

I wonder. The war in Iraq may not have ended in the ignominy of Vietnam and Afghanistan, but there was nothing that could be called victory. There was certainly no glory. The consequences of American overreach and hubris in Iraq would be felt for decades, both by those who resented US intervention and those who were called on to implement it. Kevin Powers served in the US Army as a machine gunner in Iraq in 2004 and 2005. His poetry is about moral rather than physical injury, how everyone involved in war ends up tainted.

Great Plain

Kevin Powers, 2014

Here is where appreciation starts, the boy
in a dusty velour tracksuit almost getting shot.
When I say boy, I mean it. When I say almost
getting shot, I mean exactly that. For bringing
unexploded mortars right up to us
takes a special kind of courage I don't have.
A dollar for each one, I'm told,
on orders from brigade HQ
to let the children do the dirty work.

When I say, I'd say fuck that, let the bastards find them
with the heels of boots and who cares if I mean us
as bastards and who cares if heels of boots mean things
that once were, the way grass once was a green thing
and now is not, the way the muezzin call once was
five times today and now is not

and when I say heel of boot I hope you'll appreciate
that I really mean the gone foot, any one of us
timbered and inert and when I say green
I mean like fucking Nebraska, wagon wheels on the prairie
and other things that can't be appreciated
until you're really far away and they come up
as points of reference.

I don't know what Nebraska looks like.
I've never been. When I say Nebraska
I mean the idea of, the way an ex-girlfriend of mine
once talked about the idea of a gun. But guns are not ideas.
They are not things to which comparisons are made. They are

one weight in my hand when the little boy crests the green hill
and the possibilities of shooting him or not extend out from me
like the spokes of a wheel. The hills are not green anymore
and in my mind they never were, though when I say they were
I mean I'm talking about reality. I appreciate that too,

knowing
the hills were green,
knowing
someone else has paid him
for his scavenging, one less
exploding thing beneath our feet.
I appreciate the fact
that for at least one day I don't have to decide
between dying and shooting a little boy.

Soroti, Uganda

January 1986

In early 1986, I travelled with the Ugandan rebel leader Yoweri Museveni as his National Resistance Army (NRA) took towns and villages from fleeing government forces. Amongst the NRA fighters were dozens of children, known as *kadogos*, which simply means 'little ones' in Swahili. The majority were orphans – their parents had been murdered by soldiers of the ousted president, Milton Obote. Museveni's fighters had found them wandering hungry and alone in fields of corpses. Some of the girls had been raped. Museveni said that the *kadogos* were employed only as messengers and aides, but several little boys told me they had fought and killed.

The wild violence of child soldiers has its roots in their trauma. I collected the testimonies of several whom I met in Uganda.

I saw my mother being killed by Obote's people. I watched them come to my house and kill my father. I just ran away. Then I heard that Museveni's people were collecting boys and girls, so I joined them. *George, aged fourteen*

The first thing I remember, I fall into a bush and when I open my eyes, I see a gun pointing at me. When I dream, I see animals dressed in torn clothes. They carry sticks and they chase me through the bush to the water and I keep screaming. *John, aged six*

'The soldier told me to cook food and at night he raped me. He had a gun, a bomb and a panga*. He was telling me to clean his gun and steal food from the villagers, and if I refuse I'm going to be killed. *Philomena, aged fourteen*

I fought at Katonga River. I killed one of the enemy. I felt very happy to see the enemy dying there. *Mukamba, aged nine*

Peace is a place where people are not being killed. *Matia, aged nine*

As wars proliferated across central Africa in subsequent years, children became the most feared fighters because they knew no restraint. A decade later, I met one at the airport in Goma, Zaire (now the Democratic Republic of the Congo). He must have been about thirteen, his outsized uniform hanging loosely on his skinny frame. Indicating with the barrel of his revolver, he insisted that the black boots my colleague, Tim Lambon, was wearing proved he was not a journalist but a foreign soldier. Trigger finger ready, pointing the weapon away and then back towards Tim's feet, the boy had an air of louring volatility I had never seen in an adult soldier. Tim, who could easily have knocked him down, stood motionless while, in a stammering mixture of French and Swahili, I tried to distract and dissuade the child. Even his nominal commander, who eventually managed to prise him away from us, seemed nervous.

The British-Guyanese writer Fred D'Aguiar captures the innocence of the child in the opening line of a poem that gets more menacing and violent with every stanza. The fate of his boy soldier could be that of any of the children I met in those years.

* A machete

Boy Soldier

Fred D'Aguiar, 2013

What a smile! One large lamp for a face,
smaller lanterns where skin stretches over
bones waiting for muscle, body all angles.

His Kalashnikov fires at each moving
thing before he knows what he drags
down. He halts movement of every
kind and fails to weigh whom he stops

dead or maims, his bullets
like jabs thrown before the thought
to throw them, involuntary shudders
when someone, somewhere, steps over

his shallow, unmarked, mass grave.
But his smile remains undimmed,
inviting, not knowing what hit him,
what snuffs out the wicks in his eyes.

Except that he moves and a face just like
his figures like him to stop all action
with a flick of finger on the trigger.

Wardak, Afghanistan

September 2021

Sabawoon had fought with the Taliban. A handsome, lanky man in his early forties, skin lined beyond his years, head swathed in a black turban, he said, 'We were ready for everything for the sake of Islam because our country was invaded. We didn't want to live under their rule. Our conscience would not allow us to sit at home and do nothing.'

We were in Wardak province, a Taliban stronghold. Sandbagged lookouts like medieval forts jutted from the dun-coloured hills that rose on either side of the road. Skinny goats, herded by small boys, browsed the sparse clumps of grass studding the stony earth. Every few miles, abandoned checkpoints stood testament to the failure of first the Americans and then the Afghan National Army (ANA) to exert control over the population. When we got out of the car, little girls in ragged colourful dresses and young men with kohl-rimmed eyes gathered to stare. The Taliban had returned to power in Afghanistan less than a month earlier, after the Americans abandoned the country. We were a novelty: for years, the only westerners people had seen were armed and in uniform.

It was exactly twenty years since 9/11, when al-Qaeda flew planes into the World Trade Center in New York. Many Afghans still didn't believe that the Taliban had allowed al-Qaeda to plan the attack from Afghanistan. They saw the US campaign to remove the Taliban as simply another foreign invasion of their country like that of the Russians in the 1970s and the British in the nineteenth century. Most were poor farmers as they always had been; only a quarter could read and write. Twenty years of US intervention appeared to have had little impact. Although the nearby town of Maidan Shar had elected a woman mayor in 2019, we saw no women outside. Girls went to school, but the broader western project for women's rights had scarcely reached Sabawoon's village of Alasang, even though it was only forty miles from Kabul. My Afghan friends in the capital, who had benefitted from US influence, saw the return of the Taliban as a disaster, but here people were just relieved that the fighting had stopped.

Sabawoon's father, Akhtar Gul, told us about a night in 2018 when helicopters landed just outside their house. Explosions followed, and then a raid. American soldiers, accompanied by members of the ANA, fired grenades into the house, part of which still lay in rubble. They detained Gul, who was in his seventies, for thirteen days. His brother, Sabawoon's uncle, was killed, but Sabawoon – the target of the raid – had managed to escape. The family home was attacked five times over the years, and Sabawoon's brother was killed fighting in another part of Afghanistan. It wasn't hard to understand why this family didn't see the Americans as their saviours. 'Those who brought the Americans said they would build Afghanistan, but they came here to destroy it,' said Gul.

We followed Sabawoon uphill, past the place where the helicopters had landed in 2018, towards the mountains where he had hidden from the Americans, to the family graveyard where his brother was buried. Tattered cloth flags fluttered on sticks; a dry bush had been festooned with little pieces of paper in yellow, red, pink and turquoise. Counting his bright blue prayer beads, Sabawoon squatted down in front of his brother's grave and started to cry.

Like most people from my culture and background, as well as many Afghans, I have no time for the Taliban. I hate their attitude to women and the arrogant way they impose their ultra-strict brand of Islam on other Afghans. They are cruel and intolerant. Yet at that moment, I empathised with a man mourning his brother, who believed that they had fought for a just cause.

I had spent time with US and British soldiers in Afghanistan who felt exactly the same way about their fallen comrades. The scene makes me think of Keith Douglas's Second World War poem about a soldier's need to dehumanise the enemy. Douglas was a tank commander in North Africa. 'How to Kill' shows how easy it must have been for an American soldier to 'make a ghost' of Sabawoon's brother, and for Sabawoon to throw his 'gift designed to kill' at an invader because neither saw the other as a man like himself.

You might weep for lives lost in both dusty villages and gleaming towers, I thought, for the whole sorry mess of it, and for twenty years of misunderstanding piled upon revenge.

How To Kill

Keith Douglas, 1943

Under the parabola of a ball,
a child turning into a man,
I looked into the air too long.
The ball fell in my hand, it sang
in the closed fist: *Open Open
Behold a gift designed to kill.*

Now in my dial of glass appears
the soldier who is going to die.
He smiles, and moves about in ways
his mother knows, habits of his.
The wires touch his face: I cry
NOW. Death, like a familiar, hears

And look, has made a man of dust
of a man of flesh. This sorcery
I do. Being damned, I am amused
to see the centre of love diffused
and the wave of love travel into vacancy.
How easy it is to make a ghost.

The weightless mosquito touches
her tiny shadow on the stone,
and with how like, how infinite

a lightness, man and shadow meet.
They fuse. A shadow is a man
when the mosquito death approaches.

Qaryatayn, Syria

April 2016

I never met the Islamic State fighters who fled or were killed in the Battle of al-Qaryatayn, but I did get a brief glimpse of their lives. Escorted by victorious soldiers of the Syrian government army, we were filming in the ruins of a monastery where the jihadis had murdered twenty-one Christians, when I found a notebook with an orange cover, stamped with the black seal of IS. Inside were very earthly details about pay. Why did Abu Ali al-Nuaymi receive US$200 holiday pay while Abu Mundher al-Tunisi got only US$100? We will never know. And what happened to Abu Dujanah Abu Kamal, who took a loan from the Islamic State but was already five days late with his repayments?

The details were tantalising in their mundanity. Basic pay for a soldier was US$50 per month, but Abu Khalid al-Halabi got extra because he was supporting his father, mother and two young sisters, while Abu Umar Qasir needed more to look after his disabled older brother along with three children and a wife. The notebook listed those who collected the spoils of battle and those who died. And then there was poor Abu Muhamad al-Ansari who did not attend his own wedding as he had been deployed to the tank division.

The humdrum nature of the document contrasted with the high-flown rhetoric of IS leaders. 'O soldiers of the Islamic State, continue to harvest soldiers,' the self-appointed caliph, Abu Bakr al-Baghdadi had preached in 2014. 'Erupt volcanoes of jihad everywhere!'

I wondered if the jihadis, feared and reviled across the world for their cruelty and doctrinaire subjugation of women, had grumbled as all soldiers do about rations and pay and the stupidity of their commanding officers. They had been told that their martyrdom would avenge centuries of humiliation at the hands of the Crusaders and Jews, but the Battle of al-Qaryatayn was one of scores they lost. I thought about how many victories and defeats the area had seen over the centuries. More than 4,000 years earlier, around 2300 BCE, a rebellion erupted across much of what is now Iraq and Syria as Sargon of Akkad fought to create an empire in the teeth of opposition from the old Sumerian nobles.

His daughter, Enheduana, who wrote in the ancient script of cuneiform, is the world's earliest named poet. Her hymns to Inana, an ancient deity of war, and Nanna, the daughter of the moon goddess, evoke a time of chaos and extreme violence. The fighters of the Islamic State would have recognised the images of rivers running with blood and defeated soldiers being led in chains – but would surely have been horrified to learn that the poet was a woman and the gods she venerated were female.

The Exaltation of Inana (*extract*)

Enheduana, 2300 BCE
Translated from the Sumerian by Sophus Helle

Your rage cannot
be cooled, O great
daughter of Nanna!
Queen, outstanding
on earth, who can
rob you of your rule?

The mountain fell
under your rule. Its
harvest has failed,
its city gates burn,
its rivers run with
blood – the thirsty
must drink it. All
its armies march
before you, all its
troops disband
before you, all
its soldiers stand
before you. While
the wind fills the
squares where they

danced, their best
men are led before
you in chains.

The city that did not
Say, 'This country
is yours!' that did
not say, 'It belongs
to your father!' –
the holy order has
been given: it is
back beneath your
feet. But something
is wrong with the
wombs of the city.
The woman there
no longer speaks
beautiful words to
her spouse – in the
dead of night, she
will not converse
with him. She does
not show him what
shines inside her.

LOVE

Fierce and penetrating as shrapnel

Falling in love during war is a heady experience. It's not just that the odd bomb dropping nearby makes sex especially exciting (although it does) but also the heightened sense that this might be your last moment, so you'd better make the most of it. Many wartime love affairs fail the test of peace, because the jeopardy has vanished – or because wives and husbands reappear. Yet romantic love is not the only type kindled by war. Love of country may inspire a soldier to fight, and love for comrades sustains when patriotism wanes. Love of children, and a belief in their future, motivates acts of heroism. By definition, love counters hate, and it may release people from fear. In wartime all three emotions are at their height.

Aleppo, Syria

Spring 2011

When revolution swept across the Arab world, nineteen-year-old Waad went out onto the streets with other Aleppo University students to protest against the dictatorship of Bashar al-Assad. She started to film everything happening around her. In one protest, she was badly beaten up by the riot police. She knew that if she went to hospital she might be arrested, but luckily, another protestor in her underground Facebook group was a doctor. He was twenty-three and his name was Hamza.

At first nothing happened between them; she was in a long-term relationship, and he was married. She was into politics, while he was into music and sports. Then revolution turned to war, and the Free Syrian Army took control of eastern Aleppo. Waad's parents were terrified when she said she wanted to go and live in besieged rebel-held territory. She was small and pretty with long brown hair and light-coloured eyes, and they feared what might happen to her. But she was an activist now, armed with a camera, and she had to be there. A friend drove her across the front line to a makeshift clinic in the basement of a house on the rebel side.

'I saw Hamza sleeping on a mattress on the floor, wearing his scrubs,' she recalled. Overcome with admiration for this man who was risking his life to treat fighters and civilians, she found an unexpected thought coming into her head: 'I love him.' He showed her round the front line like a tourist guide, hoping that she might stay. The fighting became more intense. Syrian helicopters dropped barrel bombs on civilian areas, while their Russian allies sprayed the area with cluster munitions. Waad and Hamza grew used to the arithmetic of survival: once you heard the roar of an 'elephant' – an improvised weapon Assad's forces made by attaching a rocket to a bomb – you had seven seconds to escape. 'A lot of people were falling madly in love,' recalled Hamza. 'It's the effect of war. At first we resisted our feelings, but then I thought, let's not waste any time because we might die tomorrow.'

The couple became part of a tight-knit group of young activists centred on Al-Quds Hospital where Hamza was director. 'It's not just two people. It's a bigger thing,' Waad explained. 'The people around us were like family.' They made a pact: she would never stop him doing his work, and he would never stop her going out to film. Documenting the war was as important as treating the wounded. And they would stay or leave together.

Somehow Waad got hold of a long white dress, a veil and a bouquet, and Hamza found a shiny mauve tie. Their wedding party took place in a friend's house, red balloons tied to the blacked-out window. Someone played 'Crazy' by Willie Nelson on their smartphone as the young couple did a slow dance. A few months later, Waad gave Hamza the good news: she was pregnant. As they walked from the hospital to the house where they were living, they heard the sound of an 'elephant'. They ran for their lives. It fell just a few metres away, on a street corner. 'You don't know what's going to happen tomorrow. You just have to make decisions,' said Waad. Marrying and starting a family was an act of defiance, an assertion of life.

Death and love were so close. Their daughter Sama was born in the hospital where Hamza treated the wounded. Thirteen hospital staff were killed in the four years they remained in eastern Aleppo. Every time they parted, even if just to go to the shops, Waad would hug and kiss Hamza as if he were never coming back.

Eventually, the brute force of the Syrian regime prevailed in Aleppo, and the rebel enclave shrank. Hamza and Waad – pregnant with their second daughter, Taima – left with Sama for Turkey in the last civilian convoy, followed by the fighters who had been given two options: leave or die.

The family lives in London now. She makes films, while he studies public health. Their love is as strong as ever. They have never abandoned the struggle for the freedom of Aleppo which brought them together.

'Until now I don't feel that we accept that we're not there any-more,' said Waad.

'Everything we went through made us the people we are today,' said Hamza.

In 'Another Place', Lisa Suhair Majaj, a Palestinian-American poet, writes about Beirut during the civil war. No one else can understand the memories that bind you to those with whom you shared such an extreme experience.

Another Place

Lisa Suhair Majaj, 2009

Who knew the past would follow us so far,
years collapsing like an ancient accordion,
scraps of memory tucked like torn photographs
into the sockets of our eyes?

Remember the gray Beirut seafront, car pulling up,
men ordering, 'Get in,' our hearts thudding against bone
as we broke and ran? Remember the splintered staccato
of bullets against rock, the way dust rose
in the stunned aftershock of silence?

Days were punctuated by static and news,
nights by the brilliance of tracer bullets
in flight. We huddled on campus steps,
transister radios pressed to our ears,
straining for some echo of the future.

That day we finally fled the beleaguered city
(tanks rolling in, danger a promise waiting
patiently) the sun sank blazing behind us
into the sea, marking a trail of blood-red light:
a path offering return.

But return was a story scribbled in a notebook
misplaced during flight. We journeyed far,
exchanged one country for another,
survived one war to live a lifetime within
others. We learned to let our faces hide
ourselves, to speak our story in a private
tongue, the past a shadow in our bones.

Salt water and sojourns leave their traces.
Decades later we hoard echoes,
still breathe the dust of that place
where banyan trees tangle
in the earth, gesticulate toward light.
Fragments of memory welter
in our flesh, fierce
and penetrating as shrapnel.

Kigali, Rwanda

April 1994

When I moved to Rwanda in February 1994 to work for UNICEF, I would hear gunshots in the night and learn the next day of killings in the suburbs of the capital, Kigali. On the night of 7th April, I was having dinner with friends when a crash sent us running into the garden. On the horizon, out towards the airport, we could see the glow of fire. The plane carrying the presidents of Rwanda and Burundi had been shot down. Within hours, the killing started. I didn't know it immediately, but this was genocide – a plan by the leaders of the Hutu majority to exterminate the minority ethnic group, the Tutsis.

The next morning, the phone in my house started ringing. My Tutsi colleagues from UNICEF were calling, asking me to save them. But I was alone in a city I scarcely knew, with no petrol in my car. Barricades manned by red-eyed drunken men armed with broken beer bottles, machetes and nail-studded clubs had sprung up all over town. What could I do? My friend Monica, the wife of my colleague, Marcel, called. He was out of the country, and their four children were safe with their grandparents in the village. They would be fine, she said, but she was going to die so would I write down her last message, how she loved them all? I got out my pen and notebook. Over the next few days I heard from Monica twice more. Then she went silent.

The weeks that followed have been well-documented. By the time the killing stopped, some 800,000 people were dead.

Monica, it turned out, was not amongst them. She had managed to hide, and then to talk her way out of danger. But there was nothing she regretted more than her survival. Her four children, and their grandparents, were dead, slain by their Hutu neighbours in the village. Their little compound in the soft green hills, the haven she had imagined, had turned into a mass grave.

A few months later, after the genocide, I accompanied Monica to church in Kigali. She sang hymns with the rest of the congregation but was wrestling with her faith. Why had God taken her children and not her? Had she not loved her children enough? How could she love Him now?

When the flames are at your back, and the instinct to protect your children at its most intense, sometimes the best option is to fling them from the burning building and into the unknown. When violence overwhelms a country, parents make unimaginable decisions to protect their children. In Nazi Germany, the poet Karen Gershon, then aged fifteen, was one of the lucky children to be packed off to the UK in 1938 by the *kindertransport* rescue operation. She didn't know until 1945, when the Red Cross published a list of those who had survived the camps, that her parents must have been killed. They had apparently been deported to Riga, Latvia, on 13th December 1941. Like Monica, she struggled with the fact of her own survival.

I Was Not There

Karen Gershon, 1961

The morning they set out from home
I was not there to comfort them
the dawn was innocent with snow
in mockery – it is not true
the dawn was neutral was immune
their shadows threaded it too soon
they were relieved that it had come
I was not there to comfort them

One told me that my father spent
a day in prison long ago
he did not tell me that he went
what difference does it make now
when he set out when he came home
I was not there to comfort him
and now I have no means to know
of what I was kept ignorant

Both my parents died in camps
I was not there to comfort them
I was not there they were alone
my mind refuses to conceive
the life the death they must have known
I must atone because I live

I could not have saved them from death
the ground is neutral underneath

Every child must leave its home
time gathers life impartially
I could have spared them nothing since
I was too young - it is not true
they might have lived to succour me
and none shall say in my defence
had I been there to comfort them
it would have made no difference

Belbek air force base, Crimea

March 2014

The first shots of Russia's war against Ukraine were fired at Belbek air force base in Crimea on 4th March 2014. A decade later, the sound would still reverberate across the world. For Ukrainian soldiers, it was unthinkable – the Russians had been their comrades-at-arms. It was the tearing apart of a military family forged over decades.

The Russian Special Operations Forces had been besieging the airbase at Belbek for five days, but Colonel Yuli Mamchur, commander of Ukraine's 204th Tactical Aviation Brigade, refused to surrender. Back in 1954, the Crimean Peninsula had been transferred from Russia to Ukraine, which made little difference as both were within the USSR. In 1991, when the USSR collapsed, Crimea became part of the newly independent country of Ukraine, but – unlike most Ukrainians – many Crimeans still felt culturally closer to Russia. Colonel Mamchur's men were Ukrainian by nationality but spoke Russian as their first language; none had ever imagined that they would have to choose which side to fight for.

On the morning of the 4th, the Russians said gas and electricity to the base would be cut if the Ukrainians did not surrender. We arrived to film the scene as Colonel Mamchur led a column of men up the hill towards the airfield, singing their regimental song. They carried not only the blue and yellow Ukrainian colours but also the banner of the 62nd Fighter Aviation Regiment that had been based in Belbek during the Second World War – an emblem of Russians and Ukrainians fighting alongside one another. To show their faith in friendship and history, the Ukrainians had laid down their weapons, but the phalanx of Russian soldiers lined up at the perimeter of the airfield was heavily armed.

As Colonel Mamchur and his men approached, the Russians raised their weapons and fired warning shots in the air. These were not only the first shots of Russia's occupation of part of Ukraine but also the first shots to be fired on the airbase since the Second World War.

'Stop! Or I'll have to shoot you in the legs!' yelled one of the Russian soldiers. The Ukrainians did not stop. When they reached the Russian line, negotiations started, and the tension eased, but the standoff continued. An hour later, Russian soldiers were still looking down their sights directly at the Ukrainians, now gathered at the top of the hill, waiting, talking, smoking – even sleeping. 'The Russians are our brothers,' one explained to me. Under Russian guns the Ukrainians played an impromptu game of football. Time ticked by.

Suddenly the atmosphere changed. Masked men appeared – not professional soldiers but thuggish-looking irregulars. They formed up in front of the Russian vehicles blocking the path to the MiG-19 fighter jets on the airfield. A few metres away, Colonel Mamchur was arguing with their leader. They said they were from the port city of Sevastopol and would protect the base. 'No,' said Colonel Mamchur, calmly. 'We will.'

Colonel Mamchur and his men held out for another twenty days. By then Russia had annexed Crimea, so the Ukrainian government ordered the withdrawal of its armed forces. The Russians arrested Colonel Mamchur but released him after three days. He had resisted for as long as possible, but now the red, white and blue of the Russian flag flew over Belbek. Forced to choose one loyalty over another, about half of the Ukrainian armed forces in Crimea defected to Russia.

Like the Crimeans, the Vietnamese had never expected to make enemies of men they regarded as brothers. Pham Ho's poem was written during the First Indochina War which pitted French colonial authorities against communists, forcing Vietnamese to choose sides. The divisions were intensified a decade later when the US intervened and Vietnam was divided into two countries, North and South. Sometimes remembering love from the past cannot save you from the hatred you feel in the present.

Beautiful and Loving Days Gone By

Pham Ho, 1950
Translated from the Vietnamese by Nguyen Ba
Chung, Nguyen Quang Thieu and Bruce Weigl

I shot him.
The beautiful and loving days gone by
Could not stop me.
Perhaps he had forgotten those days
But I remember still
The rice fields of my village, the endless sea of rice,
The morning dew like the pearls on the sides of the road,
And the two of us,
Our school books together in one bag,
Our clothes rumpled by sleep,
Our bare feet moving side by side.
In our swinging hands, the handful of rice
Our mothers rolled into a leaf of the areca palm.
Our wide conical hats had long chin straps.
In our pockets, a matchbox, a cricket inside . . .
How beautiful, how gentle the days gone by.
And yet those days held no future for us.
Many years ago
He left our village to join the enemy.
I'm sad and I'm angry.
I met him.

I shot him.
The beautiful and loving days gone by
Could not stop me.

His body lay on the dike,
No longer the boy I had known.
I looked at his face
Grieved for the boy I had lost.

Traquair House, Scotland

August 2023

Sunny Sultan had stayed in his school library in eastern Karachi late into the evening, revising for his A-levels. He was hoping to get good enough grades to go to an American university to study engineering. His Ismaili community, a branch of Shi'a Islam, were a minority in Karachi where he lived, but his grandmother lived in the US, so his dream was not out of the realms of possibility. It was 13th May 2015. He boarded the community bus at Safoora Goth, an Ismaili area, and headed home.

Saad Aziz was also on the bus. He had done his O-levels at Karachi's elite Beaconhouse school and his A-levels at Lyceum. 'He was a very hardworking child and passed with good grades,' his teacher recalled later. He went on to earn a degree in Business Administration and then open a restaurant. But that day, Aziz was dressed in a stolen police uniform and carrying a weapon. Another man guarded the bus door to prevent people from leaving, and a third shot the driver. The remaining gunmen fired into the bus for ten minutes. They killed forty-seven passengers including Sunny.

Aziz was a senior member of an al-Qaeda cell that had murdered dozens of people in Karachi. Radicalised at university, he had developed a hatred of anyone who did not adhere to his strict version of Sunni Islam or came from an ethnic or religious minority. He had spent months planning the attack on a bus he knew would be carrying Ismailis.

When Sunny's older sister, Sonal Dhanani, then aged twenty-five, heard the news she couldn't believe it. She adored her little brother. The following day, almost everyone from the Ismaili community attended his funeral, praying over the body of a boy who had shown so much promise. After the initial onslaught of shock and grief subsided, Sonal grew angry. 'I wanted to tell the world that we are a peaceful community, and we do not deserve it,' she told me. 'Then I thought, I could be angry all my life. But I have the power to change my story. So I chose love.'

Sonal decided to help both the victims and the perpetrators of violence – who, she realised, were often the same people. Karachi was the most violent place in Pakistan, plagued by political feuds as well as terrorism. Aziz, she thought, had mental health problems, so she trained as a trauma counsellor. She founded an organisation called Parindey, which means 'bird' in Urdu. 'When you have hatred, you're caged,' she explained. She went into the parts of the city where young people were being radicalised and started to talk to them. 'We reached out to vulnerable communities facing all kind of violence – ethnic, religious, even domestic.' If she had the power to change her story, she thought, then so did they.

I met Sonal at Traquair House in Scotland, where she was part of a Women in Conflict fellowship programme. Women involved in peace-building from India, Lebanon, Sri Lanka, Armenia and other countries wracked by violence had come together to share experiences and learn from each other. Eight years on, she said, Parindey – which is funded by the European Union amongst other donors – runs healing circles and trauma counselling, as well as music and art therapy. Sometimes people drop out of the programme, but Sonal has her successes, including a sixteen-year-old boy who, after a lifetime living with violence, has become a Parindey volunteer.

Saad Aziz was arrested and condemned to death for the

Safoora Goth bus attack and other acts of terror. He remains on death row. Sonal will never forget the day her brother was killed. She thinks it was anger that gave her strength and made her found Parindey. 'Killing is not easy,' she said. 'I still wonder, how could he do it? But love is easy if people can sit together. Love has great power.'

The Native American poet, Joy Harjo, often writes about the violence inflicted on her Muscogee Nation by white settlers – and how love can free you from fear.

This Morning I Pray for My Enemies

Joy Harjo, 2015

And whom do I call my enemy?
An enemy must be worthy of engagement.
I turn in the direction of the sun and keep walking.
It's the heart that asks the question, not my furious mind.
The heart is the smaller cousin of the sun.
It sees and knows everything.
It hears the gnashing even as it hears the blessing.
The door to the mind should only open from the heart.
An enemy who gets in, risks the danger of becoming a friend.

Baghdad, Iraq

December 2004

Working in warzones means losing people you love. Some deaths become emblematic of other deaths, and of the futility and cruelty of war which never achieves the results promised by those who start it. The death of our Iraqi translator, Mohammed Fatnan, haunts me still.

Mohammed had been our government minder in the time of Saddam Hussein. He was good at being bad at his job. Although he was meant to eavesdrop on our conversations and report back to the authorities, whenever I got chatting to anyone in English he would wander off. Somehow he never got round to reporting our activities to his bosses at the Ministry of Information. In the long hours we spent at the ministry, waiting for filming permits and press conferences, Mohammed would frequently disappear, but I knew where to find him. He was invariably in the communications department courting Umeima, a plump young woman with long, dark hair who operated the switchboard. It was a difficult relationship. He was a Shi'a Muslim and she was a Sunni; however much Mohammed begged, she would not broach the subject of marriage with her father.

Mohammed longed to travel and speak freely; dictatorship was stifling him and he could see no way forward other than what became known as 'regime change'. He had taken part in the failed uprising against Saddam after the 1991 war, armed not with a gun – he was the gentlest of men – but with paint thinner mixed with egg white which he used to deface pictures of the dictator. Telling us the story, he laughed at how ineffectual he had been.

Nothing bonds you to your colleagues as intensely as being under fire. It's a kind of love like no other, because you depend on one another for survival. We were at the mercy of Saddam Hussein because the British were invading Iraq alongside the Americans, so there was no embassy to whisk us to safety if anything went wrong. During the three weeks of the initial US invasion, Mohammed and our driver, Youssef, did everything to protect our news crew from Saddam's secret police, warning us when they were coming to confiscate our camera and shielding us from those who wanted to monitor our reports. The day the Americans came into town, Mohammed's round face was a picture of delight, but disillusion set in when he saw their reckless and aggressive behaviour.

One day after the invasion we spent a morning when we should have been looking for stories searching for Umeima instead. Carrying gifts, we went from house to house, but it seemed she and her parents had left town. For Mohammed, that dream was dead. Yet he was excited about living in the new Iraq. A colleague helped him get to Belgium for a two-week journalism course. Mohammed told me in wonder how he had visited the European Union and the Belgian parliament and seen how debate and voting worked.

On Christmas Eve 2004, I received a phone call from a mutual friend: Mohammed had been kidnapped. A taxi he had been travelling in from Baghdad to his home town of Kerbala had been held up by a carload of armed men on a side-road near Iskandariya. My heart sank. The US invasion had brought anarchy in its wake. With his closely shaved beard, Mohammed was very obviously a Shi'a, and the area where he had been kidnapped had become infamous for its roving bands of Sunni fighters. His parents spent months trying to establish what had happened with no success. Mohammed was never seen again.

Other friends were also killed in Iraq: the devoted aid worker Margaret Hassan, kidnapped in Baghdad and murdered by her captors; Marla Ruzicka, who campaigned for compensation for Iraqis injured by US Army actions, shot with her Iraqi co-worker, Faiz Ali Salim, as they were driving along the airport road; the distinguished political scientist Gailan Ramiz, accidentally blown up by a US bomb targeting the house next door while he was sitting in his living room. They were all family to me, because we had lived through the war together.

A million British protestors marched against the war in Iraq, but Mohammed and other Iraqi friends had convinced me that nothing could be worse than living under Saddam Hussein. They were wrong. The US-led invasion was a disaster that not only failed to bring freedom but destabilised the entire region. Mohammed was the victim of an ignorant, ahistorical intervention by outsiders and the venal sectarianism of his own society. The parallels with the American war in Vietnam are stark, not least the lives lost for a cause that seemed more tenuous with every passing day. When I think about the people I loved in Iraq, I can't help but wonder 'what if?' What if Mohammed hadn't been driving down that road that day at that time? What if someone had managed to negotiate Margaret's release? What if Gailan had been out when the bomb hit? What if Marla had taken another turning that morning? W. D. Ehrhart's poem conjures such painful thoughts from a soldier's perspective.

Beautiful Wreckage

W. D. Ehrhart, 1999

What if I didn't shoot the old lady
running away from our patrol,
or the old man in the back of the head,
or the boy in the marketplace?

Or what if the boy—but he didn't
have a grenade, and the woman in Hué
didn't lie in the rain in a mortar pit
with seven Marines just for food,

Gaffney didn't get hit in the knee,
Ames didn't die in the river, Ski
didn't die in a medevac chopper
between Con Thien and Da Nang.

In Vietnamese, Con Thien means
place of angels. What if it really was
instead of the place of rotting sandbags,
incoming heavy artillery, rats and mud.

What if the angels were Ames and Ski,
or the lady, the man, and the boy,
and they lifted Gaffney out of the mud
and healed his shattered knee?

What if none of it happened the way I said?
Would it all be a lie?
Would the wreckage be suddenly beautiful?
Would the dead rise up and walk?

HISTORY

The oranges no longer grow on his weeping groves

Wars often begin and persist because of disputed history. Israelis see the founding of the State of Israel in 1948 as a homecoming, while Palestinians regard it as the *nakba*, the catastrophe. Agreeing on a single narrative is often the most difficult part of a peace process. Every generation retells stories of victories and defeats to bolster contemporary attitudes, and adversaries start the clock of history at the moment that suits their cause. War alters not only the present but our perception of the past: after the Russian invasion in 2022, Ukrainians recast their history as a heroic struggle against the Russian imperium, while Russia produced propaganda saying Ukraine had never existed as a nation at all. Vainglorious dictators, including Vladimir Putin and Saddam Hussein, look to history to find spiritual forebears, from Peter the Great to Nebuchadnezzar II or Saladin. But all societies and governments distort history. Many Britons, steeped in a narrative of a singular heroic victory over Nazi Germany, have no idea that the Soviet Union was an ally, that some 26 million Soviet citizens – soldiers and civilians – died in the Second World War, also defending Europe from the Nazis.

Jenin, Occupied West Bank

April 2002

First it was a camp for Palestinian refugees, then a town. No – first Jenin was part of Jordan, then it was occupied by the Israelis after the Six-Day War in 1967. Actually, no. It was first a settlement of 2,307 Muslims, 108 Christians, 212 Hindus, 7 Jews and 3 Sikhs under the British Mandate. Shall we go back further? In the Ottoman period it was an administrative centre under the ruling house of a nomadic Bedouin tribe. Before that there were Crusaders, Ayyubids and Mamluks, and before them the Romans and Byzantines. Before that, in the Iron Age, it was Ein Ganim, described in the Bible as belonging to one of the Israelite tribes. Before the Iron Age, there was the Bronze Age when it may have come under the pharaohs. And so on back to the dawn of time.

When does history begin? With Israelis and Palestinians the starting point is whenever your ancestors controlled the land, or the last time you were done wrong. In Newton's third law of continuing conflict every act of violence must be met by an equal and opposite act. History, then, has no beginning and seemingly no end.

When I visited Jenin in 2002, during the second *intifada* – a Palestinian uprising against Israeli occupation – the camp had grown into an overcrowded, ramshackle town on a hill, the houses intersected by narrow stone alleyways. The then Israeli prime minister, Ariel Sharon, called it 'a vipers' nest of terror'. It was a violent time: Palestinian militants were carrying out suicide bombings at bus stops, restaurants and shopping malls in Israel while the Israel Defense Forces shot and arrested both Palestinian terror suspects and civilians. On 27th March 2002, a Palestinian suicide bomber killed thirty people and injured 140 at a Passover supper in a hotel in the Israeli town of Netanya.

The response was swift. Three days later, Israeli forces attacked the camp. We managed to sneak in just after the fighting had ended, climbing through the jagged holes that the Israeli soldiers had punched between the houses so they didn't have to expose themselves on the streets. People emerged to greet us, some holding trays of sweet tea – we were the first outsiders in nearly two weeks who hadn't come to kill them. Bodies lay under the rubble, and we could smell death even when we couldn't see it. At first we thought a body we saw in one destroyed house must have been a child, but maybe not – bodies shrink when burnt. Palestinian snipers had hidden within the warren of the camp, and the battle had been fierce – on 9th April, they killed thirteen Israeli soldiers in an ambush. After that, the Israelis had used armoured bulldozers and helicopter gunships to demolish the houses of those they called terrorists, with no regard for the families who lived there. Keep moving, people told us, don't stop or you'll be caught. We clambered over the ruins, as Israeli tanks circled below.

For Palestinians it was not a battle but a massacre. Later, Human Rights Watch concluded that fifty-two Palestinians were killed in the fighting, twenty-two of them civilians. Twenty-three Israeli soldiers lost their lives. The Israelis said they had won a great battle against terrorism.

Did it stop Jenin's young men from killing Israelis? Of course not. We saw dozens of little boys that day – I remember one, a babe in his mother's arms, maybe a year old, and another who looked about three, in red trousers and a yellow T-shirt. They have most likely grown into angry young men, without prospects, freedom, jobs or hope of an end to occupation. A few years later, they probably picked up stones to throw at Israeli soldiers, and then guns. Mosab Abu Toha grew up in Gaza, but he picked up a pen not a rifle. His poetry eloquently expresses the pain of the Palestinian dispossessed, living under occupation and war, unable to make a future as long as their history is denied.

In June 2023, Israeli forces carried out another major attack on Jenin. Both sides were better armed, the Palestinians with more automatic weapons, and the Israelis with armoured drones. The Israelis killed at least seven Palestinians. On the second day of the operation, a Palestinian driver ran down and then stabbed a group of Israelis in Tel Aviv, injuring nine. It all went back to the massacre of 2002, said the Palestinians.

My Dreams as a Child

Mosab Abu Toha, 2024

I still have dreams about
a room filled with toys
my mother always promised
we could have
if we were rich.
I still have dreams about
seeing the refugee camp
from a window on a plane.
I still have dreams about
seeing the animals
I learnt about in third grade:
elephant, giraffe, kangaroo
and wolf.
I still have dreams about
running for miles and miles
with no border blocking
my feet,
with no unexploded bombs
scaring me off.
I still have dreams about
watching my favorite team
playing soccer on the beach,
me standing and waiting for the ball
to come my way

and run away with it.
I still have dreams about
my grandfather, how much
I want to pick oranges
with him in Yaffa.
But my grandfather died,
Yaffa is occupied,
and the oranges no longer grow
on his weeping groves.

Re'im, Israel

October 2023

Sometimes Millet Ben Haim remembered the person she used to be before the music stopped. She filled her Instagram feed with images of carefree travel – in a bikini on a Brazilian beach, looking at a temple in Bali, taking a picture of a giraffe in Zambia. Always smiling. 'Cold happy days' she captioned a picture by a lake in Berlin. 'Here's to open, brave, flexible, loving hearts' on a photo with a friend in New York. She was twenty-seven.

That night she danced wildly for hours, in her shorts and crop top, flicking back her long blonde hair. The organisers had advertised the festival as a way to celebrate 'friends, love and infinite freedom'. Just after dawn the DJ pointed to the sky. At first she couldn't work out what she was seeing. Then she understood: the sky was full of rockets. Suddenly the music was cut, to be replaced by the sounds of war.

'You have those seconds of being so unbelievably happy and safe and feeling all the love,' she said. 'Half a second after that, you're running for your life.'

It was 7th October 2023, and some 3,000 young Israelis had gathered for the Supernova trance music festival at the end of the Jewish festival of Sukkot. Many of them were high, others just carried away by the music. Few saw the dark spots in the sky coming towards them – Hamas militants paragliding over the fence from Gaza, which was only three miles away. As the first gunshots whistled through the air around 6.30am, other members of Hamas were shooting the surveillance cameras on guard posts and breaking through on the ground, to embark on a rampage of killing and kidnapping in nearby kibbutzim as well as at the festival. The Israeli military, distracted by security concerns in the West Bank, failed to respond for several hours. By the time order was restored, some 1,200 Israelis were dead, including 260 of the festivalgoers. Another 240 people – mainly Israelis but also Thai workers and tourists – had been kidnapped. Pictures, some taken by Hamas, showed the bodies of young men and women scattered across the festival ground, and terrified people being abducted. The naked corpse of Shani Louk, a young German-Israeli who had attended the festival, was paraded around Gaza. She and other women were likely raped before being killed. It was the worst massacre of Jews since the founding of the State of Israel in 1948.

I met Millet and another survivor, Daniel Levii, at a therapeutic centre near Netanya three weeks later. Daniel's dark hair was partially shaved on one side. Tattoos of a magpie, a moth and a cat decorated her right arm. Bangles and hoop earrings completed the look, and she went barefoot. Millet had a silver ring through her nose and wore rolled up jeans and a white cropped T-shirt. They were from a generation of Israelis who not only looked like young Europeans but had been brought up as if they lived in Europe, not in a hostile Middle East. They embodied the dream of Israel as a safe place for Jews. In their lifetime, the Israeli government had built a huge wall – the 'separation barrier' – around the West Bank and sealed off Gaza so, although they knew Israeli Arabs, they had little interaction with Palestinians from the Occupied Territories. The 7th October attack changed all that. Now they knew they could not escape history.

Like all Israelis, their frame of reference was the Holocaust, the pogroms in Eastern Europe before that, and the expulsion of Jews from Arab countries after the founding of the Jewish state in 1948. They did not compare their suffering to that of Palestinians but to the travails of the grandparents and ancestors. Generational trauma had been reignited.

'I know that being Jewish is not safe. Period,' said Millet. 'We know we don't have any other place to go. This is our country, a place for us to live, to do whatever we want. We already tried to be in different countries, and the Holocaust happened.'

'I'm third generation here,' said Daniel. 'My grandparents built the state. We know that we can be at war in one day and the other day we can try to make peace.'

They saw the bombing of Gaza, the retaliation for the massacre they had survived, as the only way to destroy Hamas. 'I'm no longer naïve,' said Daniel, 'I don't want children and women to die, but Hamas is using them as human shields.' International support for the Palestinians filled them with fury and a sense of historical dread. 'The Holocaust happened because of propaganda,' said Millet.

They could not stop reliving what had happened that day, all the critical, instinctive decisions they had made that somehow saved their lives while others around them fell. They had been under fire for more than six hours, trying to drive away but finding cars backed up, running through open fields, crawling through bushes, hiding under leaves, all the while hearing the screams of those being killed.

'I still can't believe I'm here – it feels like a miracle,' said Daniel. 'I imagine all the time that I ran through the trees that I died – like, if I didn't do this, I would be dead, or if I didn't do that, I'd be dead. You imagine yourself dying over and over and over again.'

Millet paused as she looked for the words.

'I feel like in a way, I've died,' she said. 'I feel like a ghost.'

Such pain finds expression in the poetry of Yehuda Amichai, often regarded as the Israeli national poet. He expresses the complex emotions of a nation – the idea that the fate of an individual may be arbitrary but the Jews as a people cannot escape a history that has condemned them to suffering and trauma.

The Force of Things Past

Yehuda Amichai, 1974
Translated from the Hebrew by
Chana Bloch and Chana Kornfeld

I ask myself at what speed the force of things past
reaches me. With the velocity of melting snows
that flows from Mount Hermon all the way down to the
     Dead Sea
or a heavy slow stream of lava from an erupting volcano
or stalactites dripping in a cavern.
I do not know. On my desk there's a broken stone
with AMEN carved on it, a stone from a Jewish grave of a
     thousand years ago.
Now it's on my desk weighting down papers so they
     won't fly away,
and there it is: an ornament, a toy of history and fate.
Also on my desk there's a fragment of a hand grenade
that didn't kill me and there it is, free as a butterfly.

Kherson, Ukraine

November 2022

The priest yanked the iron handle on the trapdoor and led me down to the crypt. In the church above, old ladies in headscarves were crossing themselves and lighting votive candles: the Cathedral of St Catherine in Kherson had remained open throughout the nine months of Russian occupation so the faithful could continue to take comfort in religion. We descended a stone staircase and stepped into a small, white-washed vault where for most of the last 200 years, the bones of Prince Grigory Aleksandrovich Potemkin-Tauricheski had rested in a dark wooden coffin marked with a simple cross. Now all that remained was a rough stone dais with a candle-stand at the far end. Potemkin's coffin had been removed by a posse of Russian soldiers a few weeks earlier.

At first, said Father Ilya – a fresh-faced man in an elaborate brocaded blue and gold epitrachelion – he and other priests tried to deny the soldiers entry. Eventually there was no choice. 'They had the guns and the power,' he said. 'We had simply to obey.' Two weeks later, Russian troops who had controlled Kherson since the Russian invasion in February retreated east across the Dnipro River. They must have decided to take Potemkin's earthly remains with them when they realised that they could not hold the city through the winter – a gift, maybe, for President Vladimir Putin, who has long cited the heroes of Russian history as an inspiration for his war of imperial reconquest.

It was Potemkin who expanded the Russian Empire into what

is now southern Ukraine, founding the city of Kherson in 1778. He carried out his imperial mission on behalf of his lover, Catherine the Great, with whom he ruled almost as an equal. He was the architect of 'Novorossiya', new Russia, a concept Putin invoked in 2014 when he annexed Crimea and took control of the Donbas in eastern Ukraine. In 1783, Potemkin founded the Black Sea fleet and the naval base of Sevastopol in Crimea, which Putin's forces had seized also in 2014. It was Potemkin who presided over the construction of Odesa, Mykolaiv, Mariupol and Dnipro, cities in southern Ukraine that were now the targets of Russian shelling.

Putin said on several occasions that he did not consider Ukraine an independent country, nor Ukrainians a sovereign people with a distinct culture and history. For him they were 'little Russians' who should be reabsorbed into greater Russia. 'Their main aim is to restore the empire, and for that they use force,' said Father Ilya. 'They committed violence against those who live here because of this imaginary connection with the past.'

Milton's *Paradise Regained*, written in 1671, is about Christ's rejection of temptation, including the temptation of conquest. It can be read as a powerful repudiation of belligerent imperial ambition.

Paradise Regained
(*extract from Book III*)

John Milton, 1671

They err who count it glorious to subdue
By conquest far and wide, to overrun
Large countries, and in field great battles win,
Great cities by assault: what do these worthies,
But rob and spoil, burn, slaughter, and enslave
Peaceable nations, neighbouring or remote,
Made captive, yet deserving freedom more
Than those their conquerors, who leave behind
Nothing but ruin wheresoe'er they rove,
And all the flourishing works of peace destroy,
Then swell with pride, and must be titled gods,
Great benefactors of mankind, deliverers,
Worshipped with temple, priest, and sacrifice.

Palmyra, Syria

April 2016

Khaled al-Asaad was known as the Father of Palmyra. He was the keeper of antiquities in the ancient city – at eighty-three years of age still devoted to guarding its treasures for future generations. When the Islamic State seized Palmyra and the adjacent modern town of Tadmur in May 2015, he quietly hid as many treasures as possible. But the jihadis blew up the priceless Temple of Bel and the Triumphal Arch and took a sledgehammer to the 2,000-year-old stone Lion of al-Lāt outside the museum, so he protested. His punishment for 'worshipping statues' was death by beheading.

After Syrian government forces retook Palmyra the following year, his son, Mohammed al-Asaad, went to look for his father's body. He wept as he showed me the traffic lights in the centre of town where, eight months earlier, al-Asaad's body had been hung as an example to others. 'They brought him barefoot and told him to kneel to be executed. He refused, telling them he would die standing, like the palm trees of Palmyra which die upright and do not fall,' he said. Mohammed believed the jihadis killed his father not out of any ideological conviction but simply because they wanted to steal ancient treasures to sell.

Khaled al-Asaad's murder was reported around the world, but another person was killed that day in August 2015, someone who remained anonymous, her body lying on the road next to the traffic lights completely covered because they wouldn't show the face of a woman even in death. Her name was Fatima, and – like al-Asaad – she was tried and condemned to death in the basement of the museum which IS used as an Islamic court. Her family had fled to the nearby town of Homs, where I met them in the half-destroyed house where they were staying. Still afraid of the jihadis, her sister and mother covered their faces to disguise their identities.

'Whoever had the chance to flee didn't hesitate, but she refused, saying this is my home and I'll never leave,' her sister, Um Ahmad, told me. 'She said they were illiterate, and knew nothing, so they couldn't teach us religion or tell us to wear veils and long gowns. She wouldn't accept it.'

When the family heard that Fatima's husband had abandoned her, her mother Um Mohammed returned to Tadmur, going from office to office asking questions until one of the jihadis finally agreed to speak to her. 'He told me that we killed your daughter. I asked him why? What did she do? She is not a soldier so why kill her? He gave me a piece of paper saying she was stubborn and mocked their religion.' She showed me a document with the IS stamp which said Fatima had been sentenced to death for apostasy, for insulting her creator by questioning the wearing of the full-face veil, and for ceasing to pray and fast. In February 2021, they found the body of Khaled al-Asaad and gave him a proper burial. Fatima's body has never been found.

Religion has punished defiant women throughout history. In the Old Testament, Lot's wife was turned into a pillar of salt for disobeying the angels who told her not to look back at the burning city of Sodom. The Sri Lankan-born poet Pireeni Sundaralingam reimagines the story and – for me – evokes Fatima, the unknown woman who was killed alongside the famous man.

Lot's Wives

Pireeni Sundaralingam, 2003

We stood,
as women before us have stood,

looking back at our burning cities,
watching the smoke
rise from our empty homes.

It was quiet then. And cold.

We heard their cries, the caged birds
clawing at their perches, our daughters
naked in the hungry mob.

Such death. The smell of justice
drifting on the burnt wind.

We saw it all,
saw the fire fall like rain,

saw our tears
track stiff, white veins
down our bodies,

saw the brine crawl
through salt-cracked skin.

Now, turning in the restless night,
we dream we stand there still,
alone on the hill's black belly.

We, the forgotten,
whose names were swallowed by God.

Gračanica, Kosovo

June 1999

A few days after NATO forces entered Kosovo, a small restaurant called 1389 a few miles east of the capital, Pristina, was full of angry men. The restaurant's name was a giveaway: 1389 is the date of the Battle of Kosovo Polje, when the Serbs were defeated by the Ottoman Turks. Judging by the detail and passion with which Serbs spoke about it, you might be forgiven for thinking this historic defeat had happened in living memory, not six centuries ago. It had led to Kosovo having a Muslim Albanian majority and a Serb minority. Most Serbs I met drew a straight line from 1389 to the 1999 NATO bombing of Belgrade, which had led to this terrible moment: the surrender of Kosovo to NATO control.

The men were having a last drink before leaving their homes. They believed they had been betrayed by their government in Belgrade and by the world into another historic defeat. Their families were packed into trucks and battered cars, mattresses falling off roof-racks, children crying, women arguing, no one knowing where to go. The Serbs of Kosovo were indeed now victims – or at least losers – but they thought they had been the victims forever, that the massacres of Kosovar Albanians that had led to NATO intervention were invented, that everything was someone else's fault.

A few yards up the road, we found the Albanian sector of Gračanica deserted and destroyed. As we took pictures of the burnt-out shells of what had been homes, two Serbian women emerged from intact houses across the road. I asked what had happened to their Albanian neighbours.

'Oh, they went away during the war.'

'What happened to their houses?'

'We don't know. It happened during the night.'

'Someone must have seen . . .'

'Well, the Albanians burned down their own houses before they left.'

Both sides committed human rights abuses in Kosovo, but the overwhelming majority of murders, rapes and other atrocities were committed by Serbian police, paramilitaries and soldiers. To this day, there has been no reconciliation; Kosovars and Serbs have entirely different versions of what happened.

The 1389 Battle of Kosovo Polje took place on what the Serbs call the Field of Blackbirds. On a winter evening in Pristina a few months later, I leant out of the window of my hotel room and marvelled. A breeze was lifting the snowflakes, which appeared to be falling upwards, while great flocks of blackbirds drifted down. Sometimes, I thought, you can believe what in your heart you know to be an illusion. And – as the German Jewish poet and Holocaust survivor Günter Kunert suggests – that leaves room for history to repeat itself.

On Certain Survivors

Günter Kunert, 1972
Translated from the German by
Michael Hamburger

When the man
Was dragged out from under
The debris
Of his shelled house,
He shook himself
And said:
Never again.

At least, not right away.

COURAGE

Ah, I think there were braver deeds

Patriotic poetry and songs celebrate the bravery of soldiers, but some of the most courageous people I have come across in war have been civilians: ambulance drivers hurtling through gunfire to rescue the injured, women willing to sacrifice their own lives to protect their children from terrorists or invaders, people quietly getting on with their lives under bombardment. None of us knows how we will respond when tested, and often it's the most unassuming who find great depths of courage inside, whereas those who feel sure they would rise to the moment end up crumbling. Sometimes the greatest act of courage is to forgive, or to reach out to the enemy, when everyone around is determined to prolong the hatred that conflict engenders. War brings out the best and worst in people – courage, like love, provides a point of light in the darkness.

Butare, Rwanda

August 2013

Rose Birizihiza was not only a victim of the genocide in Rwanda, but also a witness. She did more than almost anyone to bring to justice one of the most notorious *genocidaires* – Pauline Nyiramasuhuko, the former Rwandan Minister for Women and the Family and the only woman ever to be convicted of genocidal rape.

I met Rose in her hometown, Butare, in 2013. Nineteen years earlier it had been one of the most violent and terrifying places on earth, as members of the Hutu majority set about trying to wipe out the Tutsi minority. A woman of delicate features, wearing a pink tunic and loose trousers, Rose had a strong presence, a sense of self that was rare in survivors, who had often been crushed by their terrible experiences. 'Before, I used to cry when I told my story and sometimes I couldn't finish,' she told me. 'I had many things inside me. But people encouraged me to talk because they saw how talking helped me.' Indeed, it was hard to stop the words that tumbled out of Rose, even to get her to pause for my Kinyarwanda translator to catch up. Some inner force compelled her to keep speaking.

During the genocide, a local official called Pascale Habyarimana had made Rose watch as he killed her husband. Then he took her not only to rape at will, but also to force her to provide some kind of contribution to his cause. He put her in the back of his car, drove her to where her fellow Tutsis were being tortured and murdered, and made her watch. 'I want you to see everything,' he said. 'Then when I kill you, you can go and tell the Tutsi god that Hutus are strong and have power.' Such cruelty had an unintended consequence: Rose survived and became a witness on Earth, not just against her own tormenter but also against his leader. 'Nyiramasuhuko gave the men the idea of raping Tutsi women. She had a house in town where her boys could take them. Sometimes they stripped them at her roadblock,' she told me. 'I saw people being killed in the rain at Nyiramasuhuko's roadblock. There was a hole where they would throw the bodies.'

I was especially interested in Nyiramasuhuko, because I had met her. Back in August 1994, shortly after the genocide ended, I had interviewed several victims of rape in Butare. They had told me that Nyiramasuhuko would drive around Butare in a Peugeot van with a megaphone blaring out messages calling on Hutus to fight 'the common enemy'. She would pull up in a village and stand next to her van dressed in military fatigues, giving orders to her militia – which was led by her son, Chalôme – to rape and kill. Nyiramasuhuko, they said, had escaped to a refugee camp across the border in Zaire (now the Democratic Republic of the Congo), where she was looking after orphans for the Catholic charity Caritas. I decided to chase her down and confront her.

She wasn't hard to find. A short, plump woman, wearing a sky-blue dress like the Virgin Mary in a medieval painting, she agreed to speak but not to show her face. The cameraman filmed her back. I interviewed her in French as she spoke no English. She told me that she knew nothing and had done nothing. 'If there is a person who says that a woman, a mother, killed, then I'll confront that person,' she said. I remember a sentence she spat out in anger when I provided testimonies I had heard from survivors and witnesses. '*Je ne peux pas tuer même un poulet!*' – 'I couldn't even kill a chicken!' As the atmosphere grew tense, her acolytes closed in around us, eyes burning, weapons surely somewhere close.

'Time to go,' said the cameraman. We drove as fast as we could to the border, leaving the smouldering anger of the camp behind.

Three years after our encounter, Nyiramasuhuko was arrested in Kenya and handed over to the International Criminal Tribunal for Rwanda (ICTR) in Arusha, Tanzania. Defying intimidation and death threats from Nyiramasuhuko's supporters, some of whom were still at large in Rwanda, Rose Birizihiza was one of the main prosecution witnesses. The ICTR concluded, 'Sexual violence was a step in the process of destruction of the Tutsi group – destruction of the spirit, of the will to live, and of life itself.' It had not worked with Rose. Not only had she escaped death, but her spirit and will to live were remarkably intact. Rejecting shame and silence, she also testified at courts in Canada and the USA, where *genocidaires* from Butare had fled, and in the local Rwandan justice system. Pauline Nyiramasuhuko would spend the rest of her days in gaol; Rose Birizihiza had mended her broken life through bearing witness.

Most poets only allude to such horrors, but Nick Makoha, who fled Idi Amin's Uganda as a child, does not avoid describing brutality and the tangled web of guilt that war crimes leave behind. Guilt stalks those who fail to prevent atrocities, or commit them under duress, or dare not speak about what they have seen. Few are as brave as Rose Birizihiza.

Resurrection Man

Nick Makoha, 2017

Somewhere west of our sacred sites, the ghost
of your former self is rising from captivity.
Your student friend, the one who saw you last,
swears she left you alive in the taxi. Even after my
two-fisted punches. She denies being the one who
gave the signal for dark men to change their shapes
in the night, as you knelt, blindfolded. I want to believe
she had no part in the shaving of your hair and pubic mound
in front of onlookers. Rebels kneading your breast
like posho* in their palms, begging in turn for your body,
bleached by their jeeps' headlights. Once broken,
you were dragged by the arms across the grass
onto the unpaved taxiway of Arua airport. Then
one yelled, 'Burn her! The witch.' Their echoes agreed.

One lit the match, another peeled the blindfold,
the rest poured gin on your face. I know you saw me
in the hollow of a tree, I wanted to run to you
but their bullets would have easily caught up with me.
I stood firm, learning to hide myself in the dark.
A man must have two faces; one he can live with
and one he will die with. The second face is mine.

* Maize porridge

Obiliq, Kosovo

June 1999

Commander Dini was one of the most feared officers in the Kosovo Liberation Army (KLA) – an ethnic Albanian militia seeking Kosovan independence from Serbia. Even as a child he had loved guns and hated Serbs. His real name was Abedin Sogojeva, and he cut an impressive figure – tall and strongly built, with a full black beard and long, thick curls that sprang from under his military beret. Kosovars made posters of him adapted from the famous image of Che Guevara. Three days after NATO forces entered Kosovo from neighbouring Macedonia, we were roaming around looking for a story when we crossed his path. It was NATO, not the KLA, that had defeated the Serbs, but the result was the same – here he was marching down the road in triumph with two of his men carrying the KLA flag, a black double-eagle on a red background, borrowed from the flag of Albania. You could see why Commander Dini might inspire fear, especially in Serbs, and today he was angry.

He took us down narrow dirt roads in between fields studded with scarlet poppies to a tiny settlement in Obiliq. It was a remote, desolate place – every house had been destroyed by Serbian artillery. We could hear small arms fire about a kilometre away. On a small road just outside the village, three injured men lay on filthy mattresses in two trailers. Retreating Serbian police had booby-trapped their homes. One man had tripped over a wire as he returned to his house that morning, triggering a mine that blew off his foot – the stump had been covered with a rough bandage. Two brothers in their mid-thirties were lying in the other trailer with terrible leg injuries caused by landmines that had been buried in the yard of their farmhouse. They were silent, in shock – the only sound was the buzzing of flies around their wounds. This was the era before smartphones and satellite navigation: there was no way to call for help or drop a pin on a map to tell people where we were. There were no medicines in the village, and they were afraid to go to the hospital in Pristina because the doctors and nurses there were Serbs. Besides, the tractor that pulled the trailers had run out of petrol.

We were working with two local producers: one was a Serb. Duško Tubić didn't open his mouth if we came across KLA fighters because once they knew he was a Serb they might capture or even kill him. But he couldn't keep silent, because before working as a journalist, he had been a medical student. He was terrified, he told us later, but he knew what he had to do. Tentatively, he told Commander Dini that he was a doctor. The moment he spoke the commander realised that Duško was also a Serb. Briefly, he paused. Then he nodded. Duško examined the injured men, and rebandaged their wounds tightly to ensure they didn't lose more blood. We set off in search of help.

At a nearby NATO checkpoint, Canadian troops said they could do nothing. Staff at the United Nations field hospital, which was not yet fully operational, said they didn't know the location of the village. Although returning was a further risk, while we went to edit our story, Duško guided the UN ambulance to the village to collect the injured men and bring them to the hospital. Years later, he said, 'They may have been the enemy of my state and my nation, but the men were heavily injured and in danger of losing their lives, so I had to help. It was simply my human duty.'

The American poet Stephen Crane understood that the bravery of soldiers is not necessarily the most significant form of courage in war. Duško's courage, which had its roots in compassion, cut through enmity and fear.

'Tell brave deeds of war.'

Stephen Crane, 1895

'Tell brave deeds of war.'

Then they recounted tales,—
'There were stern stands
And bitter runs for glory.'

Ah, I think there were braver deeds.

Ras Lanuf, Libya

March 2011

Were they brave or were they foolish? The uprising against Colonel Muammar Gaddafi – Brotherly Leader, Falcon of Africa and
Supreme Guide of the Great Socialist People's Libyan Arab Jama-
hiriya, amongst other grandiose titles – was both deadly and far-
cical. Protests in the east of the country quickly drove out
Gaddafi's henchmen, but a few weeks later he still held power in
the west, including in the capital, Tripoli. On the front line we
listened to the thud of artillery as his army marched down the
road towards us. Hospitals were treating young men with terrible
injuries. Some had their limbs amputated. Yet young Libyan men
did not hesitate, even though they knew the danger. They wanted
to be revolutionary heroes.

A twenty-one-year-old economics student, standing at the
side of the road looking baffled, told me he had never handled a
weapon before. The shoulder-launched rocket on which he was
leaning had 'something missing', he said. He was waiting for the
'something' to arrive but didn't seem to know what it was, nor
who would provide it. I found myself asking, in exasperation,
'Does your mother know you're here?' She did, he replied, and was
very proud of him.

Another student, this one of civil engineering, was going into
battle with no weapon at all. He reached back into his memory to
explain his logic. 'As Shakespeare says, the question is: to be or not
to be.'

'Why should I think myself better than my brothers?' added an English teacher armed simply with a kalashnikov. 'I believe that you shouldn't ask what your country does for you, but what you can do for your country.'

Such idealism, fuelled by half-remembered texts studied at school, propelled the revolution in Libya. Caught up in the beliefs that generally convince soldiers and revolutionaries – honour, patriotism, loyalty to comrades and the belief that God is on your side – they had no idea of the anarchy that would follow the demise of Gaddafi. They didn't understand that the Libyan state was hollow, and fine speeches could not fill the void. And did they really think about the impact their bravado would have on their families? The Ukrainian poet Halyna Kruk considers how a mother fears for a son who is determined to fight.

someone stands between you and death . . .

Halyna Kruk, 2022
Translated from the Ukrainian by
Sibelan Forrester

someone stands between you and death—but
who knows how much more my heart can stand—
where you are, it's so important
someone prays for you
even with their own words
even if they don't clasp their hands and kneel

plucking the stems off strawberries from the garden
I recall how I scolded you when you were small
for squashing the berries before they ripened

my heart whispers: Death, he hasn't ripened yet
he's still green, nothing in his life has been
sweeter than unwashed strawberries
I beg you: oh God, don't place him at the front,
please don't rain rockets down on him, oh God,
I don't even know what a rocket looks like,
my son, I can't picture the war even to myself

Culiacán, Mexico

December 2008

The mausoleums were as big as mansions, and the families of the dead were picnicking beneath the cupolas. Each plot sported a huge picture of the deceased, always a man between the ages of about sixteen and forty-five, touting an automatic weapon. Our guide, Javier Valdez, told us to film quickly as it was dangerous to linger in the last resting place of the *narcos*.

Javier edited a local newspaper, *Ríodoce*, carefully nurturing his contacts amongst the drug traffickers in Culiacán. The Sinaloa Cartel was at war with the Beltrán-Leyva Cartel, and the suburb where the *narcos* had lived, Tierra Blanca, was no longer pulsating with luxury vehicles and extravagant parties. Many houses were empty, their owners having quietly removed themselves to the countryside where they were less likely to be assassinated. Javier's neighbour, a member of the Sinaloa Cartel, drove us around in his huge 4x4 Chevrolet Avalanche, showing us the sights.

He pointed to a house behind massive walls where Alfredo Beltrán Leyva himself, aka 'el Mochomo', meaning 'the desert ant', had been arrested a few months earlier. Graffiti on the garage door read, 'I love you Mochomo, I miss you, your girl loves you.' We ventured into the compound. The swimming pool was half-full of fetid, green water.

We visited the shrine to Jesús Malverde, patron saint of drug traffickers, a Robin Hood-type bandit figure hanged by the

Mexican authorities in 1909. Once a simple folk-hero, he's now worshipped by those who have become rich on the profits of the drug trade. A trio of guitarist, harmonicist and singer were playing a *narco-corrida*, a praise-song to the cartels. As drugs are the foundation of Culiacán's wealth, and the war was bad for business, it was a lament.

Tierra Blanca, you seem so sad now,
Your streets are deserted,
No longer humming with the latest cars,
Nor with the roar of the machine gun.

Javier also introduced me to a *sicario*, a hitman, who called himself Miguel. He had an acute dent in his left temple where a bullet had entered his skull, and a wide, shallow one where it had exited to the right. He said he was shot by a member of a rival drug cartel who was owed US$250,000 by Miguel's boss. After thirty-two days in a coma, Miguel awoke to take his revenge. 'I was taught to return a favour,' he said. 'It was a small sin.' He was thinking of retiring, but it was hard to change career at this stage, because if your enemies don't get you then your friends will. 'You can change your phone number but your friends know how to find you,' he explained. 'I can't let them down because we're the same, we're family and you have to respect your family.'

We relied on Javier for both the story and our safety. He was one of the bravest journalists in Mexico, carefully guarding the anonymity of his sources and reporting the nefarious activities of all sides, including the police and the army. Always laughing and joshing, he seemed to be able to share a joke with everyone he met, and he had their respect. But in Mexico it's more dangerous to be a journalist than a drug trafficker. On 15th May 2017, an unidentified gunman shot Javier twelve times, a short drive away from the *Ríodoce* offices. He died on the spot. Two men were convicted of participating in his murder, allegedly on the orders of a senior member of the Sinaloa Cartel who didn't like what Javier had written about him.

The poet James Fenton, who covered the wars in Cambodia and Vietnam as a journalist, was commissioned by the BBC to write a poem to be inscribed on a monument at Broadcasting House in London in remembrance of journalists killed while reporting conflict. I think of Javier as one who 'seemed honour-bound / To take the lonely, peerless track'.

Memorial

James Fenton, 2008

We spoke, we chose to speak of war and strife –
     A task a fine ambition sought –
And some might say, who shared our work, our life:
     That praise was dearly bought.

Drivers, interpreters, these were our friends.
     These we loved. These we were trusted by.
The shocked hand wipes the blood across the lens.
     The lens looks to the sky.

Most died by mischance. Some seemed honour-bound
     To take the lonely, peerless track
Conceiving danger as a testing ground
     To which they must go back

Till the tongue fell silent and they crossed
     Beyond the realm of time and fear.
Death waved them through the checkpoint. They were lost.
     All have their story here.

Kyiv, Ukraine

March 2022

I met Olha Tymoshchuk outside an apartment block that had been hit by a Russian rocket, just down the road from where she lived. She was in her thirties, newly married, with a good job for an international company. It was only Day Twenty of Russia's 2022 invasion of Ukraine, and she was struggling to believe that her peaceful, suburban life had been shattered by war. We watched black smoke billowing out of the windows. Water from the firefighters' hoses mingled with charred dust, pouring from the balconies like blackened rain. Four people had been killed.

'It's a fifty-fifty chance,' she said. 'Either you get hit or you don't.'

The same fatalistic probability applied to Syrians hit by Russian bombs in Aleppo, and to Chechens under bombardment in Grozny in the 1990s. This was not mistargeting or rockets gone astray. Russian military strategy is to attack the civilian population to reduce morale so people encourage their government to surrender.

So what to do? Many people were leaving Kyiv for safety further west. Olha didn't want to go. She was looking after the old people in her apartment block and set against caving in – as she saw it – to Vladimir Putin. She didn't consider herself brave; it was anger that made her stay. After the Russians were pushed back beyond artillery range of Kyiv, they fired cruise missiles and Iranian-made Shahed drones into the capital and other cities. When NATO countries supplied better anti-aircraft defences, Olha, like many Ukrainians, grew inured to the siren's wail, and often didn't bother to go to the air-raid shelter. 'I sleep better at night,' she said when I met her again in June the following year. 'Sometimes I don't even hear the sirens.'

But while the odds of survival had improved, chance still played its part: you might be hit by the one missile that gets through or by shrapnel from anti-aircraft rounds. We felt it ourselves – Hotel Druzhba, where we often stayed in the town of Pokrovsk in the Donbas, and Corleone's, the restaurant next door where we often ate dinner, were hit by a Russian missile in August 2023. On New Year's Eve 2023, the Kharkiv Palace where we usually stayed in Ukraine's second city was destroyed, TV pictures showing flames shooting into the air from shattered windows. For us the odds of death were much longer, because we would spend only a few weeks at a time in Ukraine – not a lot of courage was required. But for Ukrainians who remained, being brave had become part of everyday life.

The Ukrainian novelist and poet Victoria Amelina understood the danger Russia posed specifically to writers and artists. Recalling Stalin's murder of a generation of Ukrainian writers in the 1930s, she wrote that 'there is a real threat that Russians will successfully execute another generation of Ukrainian culture – this time by missiles and bombs'. Putting aside her career as a children's writer, she concentrated on poetry and started to investigate war crimes. At thirty-seven, she was one of Ukraine's most promising writers. In her poem 'Sirens', she expresses the fatalistic feeling shared with other Ukrainians: this time it's someone else's bad luck, tomorrow it might be yours.

In the summer of 2023, she took a group of Colombian journalists to Kramatorsk, near the front line in the Donbas. They were having dinner at the Ria Pizza restaurant on 27th June when a Russian Iskander high-precision missile hit. Fourteen people were killed. Victoria Amelina suffered a devastating head injury; she died in hospital five days later.

Sirens

Victoria Amelina, 2022
Translated from the Ukrainian by
Anatoly Kudryavitsky

Air-raid sirens across the country
It feels like everyone is brought out
For execution
But only one person gets targeted
Usually the one at the edge

This time not you; all clear

LANDSCAPE

I am the grass. Let me work.

War creates its own geography. A bomb dropped by the Italian air force in the middle of the Kenyan bush during the Second World War made a crater that is now advertised as a 'natural swimming hole'. Sometimes a landscape we have never seen with our own eyes becomes associated with conflict in our minds: jungles and rice paddies with fleets of roaring choppers overhead are indelible images for anyone who has watched film footage from the Vietnam War. Shortly after arriving in Nicaragua in 1978, the photographer Susan Meiselas took a picture of a man's body, half eaten by vultures, lying near a lake in the hills above the capital, Managua. She had happened upon a place where President Anastasio Somoza's death squads dumped their victims. Twenty-five years later, she returned to the same spot and found only tufts of grass. The landscape – green, pastoral, even beautiful – gave no clue to its past. To commemorate the atrocities that had occurred there, she installed a mural-sized display of her photograph, right on the ground where the corpse had once lain. The grass grows over, but those who have experienced war are haunted by images they cannot unsee.

Ouallam, Niger

November 2021

Across the Sahel, it's not war that creates the landscape but the other way round: the impact of climate change on the land is fomenting war. People who have always lived alongside each other have become enemies. As the desert expands, herders are grazing their animals on what has traditionally been arable land, and farmers are having to cultivate ever more marginal soils. Enter the jihadis, recruiting pastoralists who have been forced to abandon their way of life and turning old land disputes into modern conflict. They control large parts of Mali and Burkina Faso and threaten Niger. Weak civilian governments have struggled to cope, and all three countries have experienced coups.

I met Safi Alferi under a flimsy straw and wood shelter in a camp for displaced people in Ouallam, a dusty town a hundred kilometres north of Niamey, the capital of Niger. She described how a violent band of men with faces swathed in cloth stormed her village on motorbikes. 'They took one person out into the bush and killed him,' she said, acting out the motions to emphasise the terror of the moment, wrapping imaginary fabric round her head and miming a rifle. 'The next day they came back and killed another. We asked them: "What do you want?" They said we must leave our village.'

Other women, dressed like Alferi in long, brightly coloured cotton wraps, most with infants jutting from their hips, crowded round to listen. A baby screeched. An old woman sitting on the sandy ground, her withered legs outstretched in front, pointed to her eyes with bony fingers to indicate that she was blind. Beyond the shelter, a relentless sun beat down. It was forty-five degrees in the shade of the sparse thorn trees. A few goats browsed amongst tattered blue plastic bags caught on twigs. I nearly passed out from the heat – it was hard to see how people would survive when it got even hotter.

In the past, such conflicts might be settled by the elders, but now jihadis are persuading pastoralists to fight under the flag of the local branch of the Islamic State. It's not difficult to see how it happens. Young men whose family herds have diminished, and who can find no alternative employment, have grown disillusioned and angry. Jihadism only has currency because their generation is looking for identity and meaning – as one community leader put it, they'd become communists if that was the ideology on offer. Also, the jihadis pay and feed them – a significant temptation in countries where government services have broken down and many go to bed hungry. Once they have joined IS, it's hard to pull the young men back into society. Not only have they killed people, but they have also burnt their neighbours' crops and houses, in a campaign of destruction to match a nihilistic ideology.

The conflict in the Sahel presages wider wars. As the climate changes, water and arable land will become scarcer in many countries. The struggle for access to resources will intensify, and greater numbers will try to get to Europe and the US. In his sonnet 'Epic', Patrick Kavanagh compares a spat between neighbours over land in rural Ireland in the 1940s to the roots of the Trojan War.

Epic

Patrick Kavanagh, 1960

I have lived in important places, times
When great events were decided: who owned
That half a rood of rock, a no-man's land
Surrounded by our pitchfork-armed claims.
I heard the Duffys shouting 'Damn your soul!'
And old McCabe stripped to the waist, seen
Step the plot defying blue cast-steel –
'Here is the march along these iron stones.'
That was the year of the Munich bother. Which
Was more important? I inclined
To lose my faith in Ballyrush and Gortin
Till Homer's ghost came whispering to my mind.
He said: I made the *Iliad* from such
A local row. Gods make their own importance.

Damascus, Syria

October 2015

Generals and journalists love maps. During the war in Syria, we would pore over online maps that charted how the front lines moved as battles were won and lost and different factions consolidated or surrendered territory until the country fragmented. What they didn't show, however, were the invisible threads that bound the country together – the bus routes.

One morning I went to the bus station in eastern Damascus and watched ten buses filling up with people about to cross the line on the map marking territory held by the Islamic State in Syria and Iraq, which the jihadis called the Caliphate. They were heading to Raqqa, its capital. Before the war the journey would have taken six or seven hours – now it could take up to eighteen. Instead of calling out the name of the next stop, the drivers would warn the passengers who controlled the next roadblock, which was especially useful for women. Those getting on the bus in Damascus were wearing loose headscarves, but on a signal from the driver they would don gloves and niqab, covering everything but their eyes. A woman had to be accompanied by a *mahram*, a male relative, but if she didn't have one the driver would pair her up with a male passenger to get through the IS checkpoints.

You could easily bribe soldiers on government checkpoints if a passenger didn't have the right paperwork, a driver told me, but that wouldn't work with the IS guards. 'Sometimes you can ask them for mercy,' he said. 'Once I quoted the Koran at them.' Some things, however, were non-negotiable. If you were bringing people out of Raqqa, IS fighters would check there were no men of military age trying to leave. 'There's nothing you can do. They take them off the bus, beat them and send them back to Raqqa.'

I watched a driver going through the luggage – if IS fighters on a roadblock found a carton of cigarettes, the smoker might be given forty lashes or gaoled for fifteen days, and the driver might also be blamed. An elderly woman with pale Bedouin tattoos on her face told me she had come to Damascus to get her pension. IS had declared that government money was *haram*, so an obliging doctor had provided a medical certificate saying she needed treatment in Damascus.

Cartography both depicts and conceals the changing reality of war. The Czech poet Miroslav Holub certainly saw the limitations of maps.

Brief Thoughts on Maps

Miroslav Holub, 1977
Translated from the Czech
by Jarmila and Ian Milner

The young lieutenant of a small Hungarian detachment in
    the Alps
sent a reconnaissance unit out onto the icy wasteland.
It began to snow
immediately,
snowed for two days and the unit
did not return.
The lieutenant suffered:
he had dispatched
his own people to death.

But the third day the unit came back.
Where had they been? How had they made their way?
Yes, they said, we considered ourselves
lost and waited for the end. And then one of us
found a map in his pocket. That calmed us down.
We pitched camp, lasted out the snowstorm and then with
    the map
we discovered our bearings.
And here we are.

The lieutenant borrowed this remarkable map
and had a good look at it. It was not a map of the Alps
but of the Pyrenees.

Ukraine

March 2022

The first thing soldiers do when a war starts is drag logs, petrol cans, rusty old cars and whatever debris they can find across the road and call it a checkpoint. Military bureaucracies invent themselves, requiring the presentation of documents that never previously existed (and may still not). Every month or so a new bureaucracy comes into being, demanding a whole new set of documents, signed and stamped.

Checkpoints embody the menace and absurdity of war: if manned by wild men with machetes or ruthless soldiers of occupation, they can be terrifying. Alternatively, they can just enable pompous blokes who have never before worn a uniform to exercise power and waste hours of your time.

In Ukraine, the checkpoint guys were looking for Russian agents and saboteurs. They were happy to see a British TV crew, not least because the British government was providing them with weapons. They were, however, curious about the grey-haired woman in the back. Our local producer, Maksym Drabok, found that three statements of questionable veracity would speed up our passing through almost any roadblock.

1) She's a very famous journalist
2) She knew the Queen personally
3) She saw Gaddafi's body with her own eyes

What gave these dubious assertions such totemic power I will never know. On one occasion, a few months before the Queen's death, the checkpoint discussion went on for several minutes until Maksym turned to me in desperation.

'He wants to know how come your Queen has lived for so long.'

'Tell him she's a vegetarian,' I replied, quick as a flash.

Of course she wasn't, but I am, and when you're asked a question at a checkpoint you have to think of something. Anyway, it worked.

Army checkpoints are not always as benign as that one in Ukraine. Ciaran Carson, who lived in Belfast all his life, evokes the scene as British soldiers erect roadblocks after rioters pelt them with 'Belfast Confetti' – improvised bombs. A familiar cityscape is transformed by a new kind of geographical punctuation. Before reading this poem, I didn't know how many streets in Belfast were named for places where the British fought in the Crimean War.

Belfast Confetti

Ciaran Carson, 1987

Suddenly as the riot squad moved in, it was raining exclamation
    marks,
Nuts, bolts, nails, car-keys. A fount of broken type. And the
    explosion
Itself – an asterisk on the map. This hyphenated line, a burst of
    rapid fire . . .
I was trying to complete a sentence in my head, but it kept
    stuttering,
All the alleyways and side-streets blocked with stops and colons.

I know this labyrinth so well – Balaclava, Raglan, Inkerman,
    Odessa Street –
Why can't I escape? Every move is punctuated. Crimea Street.
    Dead end again.
A Saracen, Kremlin-2 mesh. Makrolon face-shields. Walkie-
    talkies. What is
My name? Where am I coming from? Where am I going? A fusil-
    lade of question-marks.

Paris, France

November 2015

Blood pooling on the pavement. A bunch of supermarket red roses, wrapped in cellophane and tied to the barricades erected by the police. A pair of black and white trainers lying on the kerb. A watch with a black strap, Perspex face-cover cracked, fluorescent hands stuck at a quarter past eleven. Forensic teams in white protective suits and thin latex gloves passing a cordon maintained by police in dark blue serge uniforms who quietly keep back onlookers and journalists.

The scene after terror attacks became familiar to Europeans in the two decades following 9/11 – part of our cityscape. Back in the 1970s and 80s, the IRA carried out bombings in Britain, as did the Red Brigade in Italy, but the jihadi campaign linked to al-Qaeda and IS has been more widespread and more lethal. For foreign correspondents, covering terror attacks at home became routine. If you thought about it too much it was unnerving, so on the whole we didn't. We just got on with reporting.

The bombings in Paris on 13th November 2015 were amongst the most deadly. That evening, 130 people were killed and more than 400 injured. At 9.15pm, three attackers blew themselves up outside the Stade de France where a football match between France and Germany was underway. Another group fired on people sitting in cafés and restaurants. A third raided the Bataclan theatre where The Eagles of Death Metal, a rock band from California, were playing. They shot wildly into the crowd and took the rest of the concert-goers hostage for several hours. Seven suicide bombers killed themselves; another two were shot by the police two days later.

When we arrived at the Bataclan the following morning, some of those who lived nearby were wandering around, still in shock, as if returning to see the debris in the light of day somehow made more real what they had witnessed. 'People were bleeding and yelling. We helped them,' said Ismène Ahmed, who had rushed to the scene from her nearby apartment. I asked if she had figured out what was going on. 'Yes, we understood. It was an attack. It couldn't be something else. It was terrorists. We were being attacked again.'

Most of the bombers were of Moroccan or Algerian origin but had been born in France or Belgium. Two were Iraqi. Several had been radicalised in Europe, and had been amongst the more than 3,000 Europeans who had travelled to Syria to fight alongside IS. So who was exporting terrorism to whom? Was it infecting the Arab world from Europe, or Europe from the Arab world? War was no longer something that happened in far-off countries of which we knew little – it was bubbling up from within.

We visited a hospital where people queued to give blood. A young woman and her brother told me they were looking for a friend whose parents didn't yet know he was missing. By the time we returned to the Bataclan, more people had gathered. They laid flowers and lit candles. Someone had brought a piano, and a young man played John Lennon's 'Imagine'. Yehuda Amichai's poem shows how a terror attack has an impact far beyond its immediate environs, whatever the cause of the bomber or the nationality of the victims.

The Diameter of the Bomb

Yehuda Amichai, 1976
Translated from the Hebrew by
Yehuda Amichai and Ted Hughes

The diameter of the bomb was thirty centimetres
and the diameter of its effective
range - about seven metres.
with four dead and eleven wounded.
And around them in a greater circle
of pain and time are scattered
two hospitals and one cemetery.
But the young woman who was
buried where she came from,
over a hundred kilometres away,
enlarges the circle greatly.
And the lone man who weeps over her death
in a far corner of a distant country
includes the entire world in the circle.
And I won't speak at all about the crying of orphans
that reaches to the seat of God
and from there onward, making
the circle without end and without God.

Nyakisu, Rwanda

April 2013

For years, the rainy season would bring up bodies that had lain where they were slaughtered. You might see clothes floating in a flooded field or stumble across a leg bone or a child's skull half covered in mud. Nowadays, the rain lifts memories to the surface. It beats down on iron roofs like a manic drum, conjuring demons that Rwandans suppress for the rest of the year. Pastors, counsellors and doctors open their doors to find people they haven't seen for months complaining of unspecific pains and worries, sleeplessness and headaches. Rain pitches them back to the second week of April 1994 when the sky opened up like a vast cataract and the killing started.

My own memories of that week are fragmented, like a reel of old film with some frames missing. I was living in the Rwandan capital, Kigali, working temporarily for UNICEF. I lay in my bed at night listening to the sound of rocket fire, but it was the quiet times that were most terrifying. That was when the killers were at large. I saw how rain diluted the blood running in the gutters. When I travelled into the countryside, I found bodies lying in ditches. The churches were full of skeletons and rotting clothing. Today's tourism brochures describe Rwanda as 'a land of astonishing beauty', but in my mind the fold of every green hill conceals an atrocity, like sumptuous paintwork over bloodstains on the walls of an elegant palace. Rwanda's stunning geography is used to boost government propaganda that Rwandans live in harmony in a pastoral idyll and no longer fear the neighbours who killed their parents and grandparents.

In 2013, I visited the village of Nyakisu, near the southern town of Butare where, nineteen years earlier, members of the Hutu majority had murdered their Tutsi neighbours. The Rwandan government had banned people from saying 'Tutsi' and 'Hutu', as if the abolition of words could abolish the emotions they contained. Stall-holders were laying out plastic plates, blocks of soap and batteries, all the basics of life in rural Africa. In the bar across the red dirt street, a few men were sitting on benches drinking Primus beer from the bottle.

I was waiting for Viator Kambanda, who arrived on a borrowed bicycle painted red, green and yellow with the legend GIKURUNDU, meaning 'Something Beloved'. A cobbler by trade, he said most people in the area were too poor to get their shoes mended. His own were made of plastic, repaired with crude stitches. He wanted to go to Kigali to look for work but couldn't because the authorities wouldn't give him an ID card. Life was especially hard for him, he said, because he had spent nine years in prison and was yet to complete his community service. Viator didn't want anyone to see us talking, so we agreed to meet half an hour later at a glade of eucalyptus trees above the village.

Dappled sunlight streamed through the branches as we sat on the grass. I asked what he had done in the genocide. 'It was my first time to kill so I was scared,' he said. 'Her name was Kandida Nyiramakonze. She was my neighbour.' He had run with the pack, just one amongst a horde of killers. 'There were many Tutsis in a group. I called her name and told her to sit down. Then I hit her on the head twice with a big stick and she died.'

A small cream and purple orchid was growing amongst the coarse grass. A yellow butterfly flitted past. Viator had been released after confessing and expressing remorse at a local trial in 2008. I asked why he had killed Kandida. 'I wanted to save her so they couldn't kill her in a worse way or even rape her. Someone else killed four children and her husband.' Schoolchildren walked past on the road above, shouting and giggling. I looked across the valley to the next hillside, clad in a dozen shades of green, studded with little red houses with drainpipe roof tiles. White clouds stacked up in a bright blue sky. It was like a child's painting of an idealised countryside. 'It was not easy because you would see a person cutting someone with a machete when you might have been with the victim the evening before,' said Viator. 'I was not angry at the Tutsis. We lived well together before. I even loved them, but our leaders encouraged us to kill.'

In its public statements, the Rwandan government acts as if the grass has grown over – in Carl Sandburg's image – as if the rains just make the landscape greener without bringing anything to the surface. But the graves in Rwanda are shallow. I asked Viator if hatred was still an issue in Nyakisu. 'If we're alone we can say what we like – I could even say bad things about a Tutsi,' he said. Talking in a public place was quite different. 'You can't say those words,' he said. 'They'll just kill you.'

'Which words?' I asked.

'Words like, "Let's finish the job."'

'Do people want to say those words? Do you?'

He stared into the distance for a long time. I could hear the trill of birdsong. 'People here are ignorant,' he said eventually. 'If we had known there was no Hutu and no Tutsi we wouldn't have done the genocide. But those feelings are still here.'

Grass

Carl Sandburg, 1918

Pile the bodies high at Austerlitz and Waterloo.
Shovel them under and let me work—
        I am the grass; I cover all.

And pile them high at Gettysburg
And pile them high at Ypres and Verdun.
Shovel them under and let me work.
Two years, ten years, and passengers ask the conductor:
        What place is this?
        Where are we now?

        I am the grass.
        Let me work.

PRISON

They cannot snuff out the moon

Dictators always lock up their opponents – it's the easiest way of silencing them. But those living under occupation are also prisoners, unable to travel freely to and from their own land, or to live where they choose within it. While fighting or waiting for freedom, prisoners have to learn how to live without it, to find a kind of liberty in their own mind to stave off despair or madness. Some develop Stockholm Syndrome and cannot cope with freedom. The joy of release rarely lasts, as a new dictator takes power, or the challenges of peace prove insurmountable. But one of the greatest privileges of being a journalist is to experience the moment of liberation with someone, to feel that glorious sensation even if it lasts less than a day.

Hasharon Prison, Israel

January 2006

'The Israelis succeeded to arrest my body, but not my head, not my soul,' said Marwan Barghouti. He was speaking in the tiny cell he shared with two other Palestinian prisoners. Such was his popularity and political importance, I thought that the next time I saw him, he might be the Palestinian president, but history took a different turn. Barghouti has spent more than a third of his life in prison. He has not even been allowed to give another interview. To the Israeli government, he's a terrorist, convicted on five counts of murder. To Palestinians he's a hero, their Nelson Mandela.

I first met Barghouti in the West Bank town of Ramallah in 2001 during the second *intifada*, or uprising. Israeli settlements were expanding further into Palestinian land. Palestinian militants were carrying out terror attacks in Israel, while others battled Israeli soldiers in the West Bank. The youths lobbing rocks at Israeli soldiers in Ramallah towered over Barghouti, a small, stocky man in a leather jacket, but the crowd always parted for him. His charisma was apparent.

The muezzin wailed through the white-washed prison block. After three years in solitary confinement, Barghouti, then aged forty-six, was living with 118 other Palestinian prisoners. Each cell had a blue metal door and bars across a narrow window overlooking a courtyard. Dressed in a brown prison uniform, Barghouti was talking to other prisoners outside his cell; normally he was locked in for twenty-one hours a day. I introduced myself. He turned his back, uninterested.

'I saw your wife yesterday,' I said.

He swung round. 'Where? How is she doing? Is she all right?'

'She's doing well,' I said.

I had met Fadwa Barghouti as she was campaigning on his behalf in upcoming Palestinian elections in the West Bank. The Israelis had agreed to the interview because they thought Barghouti might persuade Palestinians to vote for the more moderate Fatah rather than the Islamists of Hamas. (Fatah won in the West Bank, Hamas in Gaza.)

Barghouti invited me into the cell, and we sat on his low bed opposite the bunks where his cellmates slept. Pictures of his family were taped to the walls: Fadwa and his four children, including his eldest son, Qassam, also in gaol. From a box under the bed, he pulled out books in English, Arabic and Hebrew, all of which he speaks fluently: tomes on the Middle East – Dennis Ross, Edward Said – poetry by Mahmoud Darwish, the writings of Paolo Coelho. He was studying leadership, reading the memoirs of Bill Clinton and Margaret Thatcher and the most recent Hebrew biography of his nemesis, Ariel Sharon. 'We need two leaders who are ready to take decisions, and to take risks on both the Israeli side and the Palestinian side,' he said.

The most famous picture of Barghouti was taken at his trial in 2002 in an Israeli court which he refused to recognise. Smiling at his supporters, he raises clasped, cuffed hands, the chain dangling from his wrists. It's an image reproduced in murals across the West Bank. Although Barghouti led the Tanzim, the militant wing of the late Yasser Arafat's Fatah movement, he denied targeting civilians. 'Believe me, the Israelis consider everybody against occupation is a terrorist,' he said. 'It's not true. No one can justify killing civilians – children, women, anywhere in this world.' He was optimistic. 'They will not break our will for independence and for freedom,' he said. 'I will be free with all these prisoners.' In the end, he said, the South African apartheid regime negotiated with Mandela, and the British talked to the IRA.

Since the interview, Barghouti has been moved several times to different prisons. Other inmates call him 'professor' because he has read so many books and organises study sessions. His family are allowed to visit only occasionally. In 2024 I met his son, Arab, who was 11 when his father was arrested. He has only been allowed to visit every two or three years, always separated by a glass screen. He looked at me with envy. 'I haven't touched him since 2002,' he said. 'You probably shook his hand, but I wasn't able to.' Nor has Barghouti met his six grandchildren. Arab wasn't sure how much his father knew about the Hamas attack on Israel in October 2023, and the subsequent relentless Israeli onslaught on Gaza. His lawyer, who has visited since then, told the family that a prison guard had dislocated Barghouti's shoulder when he refused to put his hands behind his back. He was struggling to see out of his right eye after one assault, and was unrecognisable from the defiant images reproduced on murals. Barghouti had been returned to solitary confinement, without electricity or basic hygiene. The cell window had been blocked. The Israeli authorities, under a far right national security minister, not only arrested hundreds more Palestinians, including non-violent protestors, but appeared to have told the prison guards to take revenge on prisoners for the atrocity Hamas had committed.

As we left Hasharon, I talked to one of the Israeli prison officers. 'Before I worked here, I only saw Palestinians through the sights of my gun,' he said. 'But here I talk to them, especially Barghouti. I think he's a terrorist. I disagree with him. But in the end he must be released. You make peace with your enemy not your friend.' I cannot imagine an Israeli prison guard saying that now, nor Barghouti maintaining his faith in the future.

In 1951, the Pakistani journalist and poet Faiz Ahmed Faiz was arrested, accused of plotting to overthrow the government. He spent four years in prison, the first of several periods of incarceration. Prison guards sometimes smuggled in pen and paper so he could write poetry. He staved off despair by looking at the sky at night and thinking of how his gaolers could not control the natural world. I wonder if Barghouti finds comfort similarly, or whether the thoughtfulness and optimism that both his gaoler and I saw in him has been extinguished by the long, unforgiving years of incarceration and the despair that characterises the Middle East today.

A Prison Evening

Faiz Ahmed Faiz, 1952
Translated from the Urdu by Agha Shahid Ali

Each star a rung,
night comes down the spiral
staircase of the evening.
The breeze passes by so very close
as if someone just happened to speak of love.
In the courtyard,
the trees are absorbed refugees
embroidering maps of return on the sky.
On the roof,
the moon – lovingly, generously –
is turning the stars
into a dust of sheen.
From every corner, dark-green shadows,
in ripples, come towards me.
At any moment they may break over me,
like the waves of pain each time I remember
this separation from my lover.

This thought keeps consoling me:
though tyrants may command that lamps be smashed
in rooms where lovers are destined to meet,
they cannot snuff out the moon, so today,

nor tomorrow, no tyranny will succeed,
no poison of torture make me bitter,
if just one evening in prison
can be so strangely sweet,
if just one moment anywhere on this earth.

Baghdad, Iraq

April 2003

The colonel had long wanted to shoot Saddam Hussein and this was his chance. He pulled the 9mm pistol from his pocket and aimed. The first bullet hit the dictator in the torso. The second in the head. 'Now I feel better,' he said as he re-holstered his weapon.

American forces had taken Baghdad a few days earlier, forcing the Iraqi dictator and the remnants of his regime to flee. We were at Abu Ghraib prison, where thousands of Iraqis had been held and tortured. The colonel had been wandering around, looking for someone to witness the act of revenge he was about to commit. He took us to a huge mural, where Saddam was depicted in a shirt and tie with dark glasses, surrounded by his adoring subjects, some raising their arms in praise. 'I took part in building this wall,' he explained after he had shot his nemesis. 'I was a political prisoner here for five years. It's personal. I came to wash away the shame.'

The colonel told us that his imprisonment was punishment for taking part in a failed coup. Having been forced to create a monument to the man he hated more than any other, the wall was a symbol of his humiliation. He was lucky to be alive; he showed us the gallows where hundreds had been hanged. A noose had been flung onto the floor by other former prisoners who had also returned to the scene of their persecution.

I still carry with me one of the colonel's bullets that ricocheted from the concrete wall – a small round flattened piece of metal like a button – a symbol of the human need for freedom. The Syrian poet Mohammed al-Maghout – seen as a pioneer of free verse in Arabic – also spent time in prison, writing poetry on cigarette papers. Throughout his writing, his humour asserts his humanity in the face of totalitarian oppression, breaking through the prison walls to connect with the reader.

The Compulsory Reasons

Mohammed al-Maghout, 2001
Translated from the Arabic by Noel Abdulahad

Whenever freedom rains anywhere in the world,
Arab regimes rush to cover people with umbrellas,
fearing that they will 'catch cold.'

Why do Arabs apparently cling to anything and everything?
Are they about to drown?

With everything around us cracking and collapsing,
Where lie the ruins?
Did they sell them already?

All face collapse;
all want to shore each other up.

Whenever two Arabs meet,
intelligence services make a third.

With your hands trembling,
you cannot hit any target.
Whatever sky they circle,
Arab clouds and Arab planes

war with each other, and their surroundings,
like all Arab communities on earth.

Martyrs fall on sidewalks,
While despots march in roads.

And any Arab unity
lies in mass graves.

When people have nearly ceased to believe,
their leaders have become the pious faithful.

Al-Hol, Syria

March 2019

Khadija was twelve years old and my appearance horrified her. 'Why isn't she wearing Islamic dress?' she asked the women around her. I had covered my head with a scarf, but that wasn't enough. Khadija had been living in the Islamic State Caliphate for five years, and in her eyes any woman who wasn't dressed head-to-toe in black in public might as well be naked.

We were in al-Hol camp, where Kurdish fighters had confined some of the 70,000 women and children they had captured during the final battle to destroy the Caliphate. It was a bleak place. A cold wind whipped along the sandy soil, filling with grit the blankets and washed clothes the women had hung on the wire fences that imprisoned them. The Kurdish female guards, dressed in military uniforms and bright floral scarves, saw the IS treatment of women as oppressive, but the women of al-Hol didn't think they had been liberated. The final battle had taken place in a small desert town called al-Baghuz where the remnants of IS had fled from Raqqa, the capital of the Caliphate. The Kurds and their American allies had relentlessly bombarded the fighters and their families, who limped out in small groups, leaving only the most tenacious fighters to perish rather than be captured.

The women might have surrendered physically, but psychologically they remained fanatical supporters of IS. 'The Islamic State will last forever and this will be proved in the coming days!' yelled a forceful middle-aged woman, swathed in black cloth, who refused to tell me her name. 'I swear to God, it was brilliant. There was no food but the women were proud. All women were sisters – one heart, one religion.' I wondered if she had been part of the Al-Khansaa Brigade, an armed all-female IS unit that enforced the strict dress code and other rules that ensured women remained subservient to men.

I went to talk to a painfully thin woman, whose shoulders were jutting through her abaya like broken wings. All I could see of Yasmina Haj Omar were her eyes, one of which had a squint. She told me that when she was thirteen, IS fighters had arrived in her village near Aleppo and taken her with them when they moved on. Now aged nineteen, she had been married four times to foreigners and twice to Syrian fighters – six husbands in as many years. Each time a husband was martyred – in other words, killed in battle – she was passed on to another.

'How do you feel about that?' I asked. 'It was fine because I was following the word of the Prophet,' she replied. 'All of this is for the glory of God.' Yasmina complained that she felt weak, had been unable to have children and suffered persistent vaginal bleeding. The ills that befell her, she explained, were caused by the Americans, who had not only pursued her and her husbands from place to place with their aerial attacks but also sponsored the Kurdish forces. 'I was injured in the womb by bombing,' she said. If it had occurred to her that being handed on from one man to the next might have caused her gynaecological problems, she did not show it. She may have been a prisoner of the Kurds, but her real gaolers were the jihadis who had captured her mind and destroyed her body. How easy it is for the oppressed to take on the ideology of their oppressors.

The poet Andrew Waterhouse's bleak vision of an occupied city, with its shackled women and bearded men, makes me think of Raqqa. Some women in al-Hol had absorbed the jihadi vision, but others just kept their heads down, trying to survive the imposition of a brutal, alien ideology, looking nervously behind and above.

Now the City has Fallen

Andrew Waterhouse, 2000

The radio station is filled with goats,
all telephone lines recoiled to their source,
the city gates closed and locked for the last time.

Women are shackled and painted red
the men given false beards and new names;
I am He Who Looks Nervously Behind,
my friend is He Who Looks Nervously Above.
They want us all to be very nervous.

The firstborn of a firstborn has to give
an organ for God. The rich buy poor men's livers
from secret markets. There is never a shortage.

All trees are being felled as they keep heaven
from earth. The invaders only eat human flesh.
Our children are taken from us and reared
in darkness. It is unclean to wash the body,
only the soul can be touched and scoured bright.
It must be left out on the roof tops for the sun and moon.
    This is the law.

We sit each evening and talk about them;
their strange ways are mysterious to us.
We do not know where they come from.
We only know that they are with us.

Sderot, Israel

November 2023

We stood on the hill overlooking Gaza, watching the bombs fall and turning people into statistics: 560 dead; 7,028; 11,100. As the weeks went by the tally grew – the 37,000 cited by the Gaza Health Ministry in mid-June was probably an underestimate because no one knew how many bodies lay under the rubble. The people of Gaza were being punished for atrocities committed by their rulers, Hamas, who had stormed the Israeli border to kill and kidnap Jews on 7th October. The ratio was two to one, said the Israel Defense Forces – two civilians killed for every Hamas fighter.

Even before the war, Gaza was the world's largest prison. Two million people are confined to a strip of land forty-one kilometres long and six to twelve kilometres wide, allowed to leave only with Israeli or Egyptian permission, which is rarely granted. The Israelis withdrew their settlements in 2005 but still control the borders, coastline and airspace. In 2007, after the Islamist group Hamas came to power – refusing to recognise the Jewish State and committing sporadic terror attacks – Israel blockaded the territory.

Gazan civilians found it hard to live decent lives. Every time I visited, I felt their frustration and anger rising – it was less the poverty and unemployment, and more the feeling of being trapped, of having no control over their lives, the humiliation of being subject both to the strictures of Hamas and the political whims of an increasingly harsh Israeli government that refused to see the humanity of Palestinians.

One of the few who did manage to get out was Dima Alhaj, who spent a happy year at Glasgow University in 2019, on a scholarship to study Environmental Science. 'Dima loved Glasgow,' said Roseann Maguire, who hosted her. 'She embraced the freedoms that she had here, which she didn't have in Gaza because of the siege.' She and her friend, Nagam, enjoyed walking around the city and chatting to people. She even became a Celtic fan. She dreamed of travelling again one day, maybe to do a PhD, but her future lay in Gaza. She and Nagam would giggle with Roseann about the young men they knew back home. She returned willingly. Some time later, Dima sent Roseann and her husband, Gerry, a message saying she was about to marry. She had got a good job with the World Health Organization at a centre for Gazans with limb injuries (mostly caused by Israeli bullets). And then came the best news of all – she had given birth to a healthy baby boy, Abdel Hakim. She sent the family in Glasgow pictures by WhatsApp. 'The baby had her smile,' said Roseann.

The WhatsApp messages continued through the first weeks of the 2023 Israeli assault, as Dima and her little family were forced to move four times to escape bombardment.

'Dear Roseann, the situation here is really tough. We're trying our best to stay calm and safe.'

'I can see the support coming from the Celtic fans!'

'Pray for us.'

'This is about my little boy. I hope he lives to see better days.'

That was the last message.

At 4.20am on 21st November 2023, Dima Alhaj was killed by an Israeli airstrike. She was twenty-nine. Her husband and five-month-old baby were killed with her, alongside some forty members of her extended family. They had all been sheltering in the house of her father, Dr Abdelatif Alhaj, which took a direct hit. As one of Gaza's senior surgeons, he was at the hospital that night. A week later, he returned to survey the wreckage of the home where he and his wife, Aya, had raised their five children, three of whom were now dead. He stood in the wasteland of rubble that had been a garden full of flowers and trees where he remembered Dima used to rock baby Hakim. 'It seems the Israelis don't like anything beautiful in Gaza,' he said. Spotting something white, he reached down into the ruins and pulled out Hakim's bib. He raised it to his nose. 'It still has the baby smell.'

I witnessed this heartbreaking scene because a Palestinian journalist, Yousef Hammash, filmed it for a TV story I put together. Israel would not allow foreign journalists into Gaza during the war, and we had struggled to tell the stories of individual Gazans. Dima, with her smiling face on a poster at a vigil at Glasgow University, was one of the few who wasn't just an anonymous white-shrouded corpse or a crushed body on a TV screen. The images of injured children covered in blood and dust, and the number of deaths, sparked horror and outrage, but Dima was someone viewers could mourn.

In his poem 'Mourning Problems', the Chinese poet Xi Chuan questions who and what we mourn and why, and what is left of us.

Mourning Problems

Xi Chuan, 2014
Translated from the Chinese by Lucas Klein

an ant dies, and no one mourns
a bird dies, and no one mourns if it isn't a crested ibis
a monkey dies, and monkeys mourn
a monkey dies, and people pry open its skull
a shark dies, and another shark keeps swimming
a tiger dies, and some people mourning are mourning
    themselves
a person dies, and some people mourn and some
    people don't
a person dies, and some people mourn and some even
    applaud
a generation dies, and the next generation doesn't really
    mourn
a country dies, most of the time just leaving apocrypha
a country that doesn't leave apocrypha wasn't a real country
if it wasn't a real country, when it dies no one mourns
no one mourns, and the wind blows in vain
rivers flow in vain, washing over rocks in vain
glistening in vain, making vain ripples
the river dies, and it's not for man to mourn
the wind dies, and it's not for man to mourn

the river and wind make their way to the sea, the sea as vast as
    in the Zhuangzi*
the vast sea dies, and you will have to die
the dragon king dies, and you will have to die
the moon doesn't mourn, there's no one on the moon
the stars don't mourn, the stars aren't flesh and blood

* The Zhuangzi is a huge collection of Daoist philosophical writing from the
fifth to the third century BCE.

Gao, Mali

January 2013

The sun was rising as we hurtled into the city of Gao on the back of a Malian army pick-up truck.

I had never seen such excitement. People on motor scooters roared around us like manic outriders. Perilously steering with one hand, some raised beer bottles to their lips – after nine months of enforced teetotalism, at last they could have a drink! It was a moment of absolute joy. Islamists of the Movement for Oneness and Jihad in West Africa (MOJWA), who had occupied the town, had been driven out by the national army, supported by the French. Cheering pillion passengers held aloft the Malian and French colours – for this brief period, the old colonial power was seen as a liberator not an oppressor.

Such happiness could not last, but it was hard not to get caught up in it. Everyone wanted to show us around, to tell us their story. After effective imprisonment, the chaos was glorious. Soldiers took us to a clearing where MOJWA operatives had flogged those who drank alcohol or smoked; the sand was black where they had stamped on the offending cigarettes. It was outside the mayor's office which had been used as an Islamic court. Inside, the floor was littered with documents outlining Sharia statutes and rules. After the jihadis fled, local people broke in. Aramatou Cissé, dressed in the kind of traditional colourful wrap that the jihadis had banned in favour of all-encompassing black, told me she had been arrested for the crime of riding a motorbike while female. 'I was on the road, and they were behind me,' she explained. 'They hit me with their car. Then they took me to the police station and shaved my head.'

We went to visit her aunts and sisters who were sitting chatting in the dusty courtyard of their house. Most Malian women wear bright headscarves mainly as protection from the sun; they follow a form of Islam that does not oblige them to cover their heads nor to follow the strict gender segregation that the jihadis had imposed. The men of MOJWA, who were mostly Arabs, had banned women from dancing or singing, and even from wearing glasses. Why? 'Because they didn't want us to see the world.' Forced to obey what they regarded as ridiculous rules, the women had never allowed themselves to despair or to stop hoping that one day they would be liberated. They pulled scarves over their heads and tore them off to demonstrate how they had been forced to cover up but could now show their faces. And in this brief, wondrous moment of freedom, they laughed and laughed.

Nibha Shah is a Nepali poet who was imprisoned for ten months in 2003 for fighting with Nepal's Maoist rebels. She writes not only in defiance of her imprisonment, but in defiance of any attempt to contain women and restrict free thought.

Cage (2002)

Nibha Shah
Translated from the Nepali by
Muna Gurung

We want
eyes to open:
eyes will open
We want to live free:
Who can cage us?

We look at the faces of
light and darkness–
light pierces darkness.

Your walls couldn't cage us
Even inside the prison, we continued to fly
carrying feathers of ideas,
Even inside the prison, we continued to burn
with the light of faith
Now say, where will you cage us?

Your handcuffs and nails couldn't cage us
Your beatings couldn't shrink us
We tore into shreds your

forms for surrender
We signed off on your
standard procedures for death
Now say, where will you cage us?

CHILDREN

Child of our time, our times have robbed your cradle

Nothing brings home to people more starkly the horror of war than a child being killed or maimed. Sadly, journalists find there is never a shortage of such stories. According to the Peace Research Institute Oslo, about 468 million children – more than one in six – were living in a conflict zone in 2022. This number has almost doubled since the mid-1990s. Being killed in crossfire or bombing is the least of it. In Africa and the Middle East, where conflict often destroys already inadequate health facilities and forces millions to flee to camps in equally impoverished neighbouring countries, children are especially vulnerable. War overturns the western notion of childhood continuing into your teens. When children are orphaned, or forced to work as soldiers, couriers or informers, they grow up very quickly.

Baghdad, Iraq

March 2003

It was the day after US tanks had rumbled into Baghdad and Saddam Hussein's forces had melted away. Iraqis approached the Americans with sweets and bouquets of flowers; as the US administration had predicted, they were greeted as liberators.

We were heading to Adhamiya Palace, which had been occupied by US marines and where we heard there had been a gun-battle. It was quiet as we approached, but we knew the Yanks could be trigger-happy so we parked some way off and walked up calling out 'British television!' I carried a white flag made of one of my scarves tied to a broomstick. The marines on the gate wouldn't let us in. They said that earlier that morning they had been fired on from the mosque opposite and thirty-eight of their number had been injured. We waited. Marines situated on the palace walls above us fired sporadically at threats, real or imagined. They had erected no signage, so a bullet was the only way anyone could discover that the road was closed. A blue Passat drove along the road opposite and disappeared round a corner. A volley of gunfire rang out from above. Silence. And then the faint sound of crying.

Our translator, Mohammed Fatnan, told the marines he was going to see what had happened so they had better not shoot him. He ran across the road. After a few minutes, he ran back carrying a bundle in his arms. The next few moments are seared in my memory: as he got closer I could see the bundle was a little girl in an orange-and-white spotted dress, with long dark curly hair. Her name was Zahra. She was six years old. The marines had shot her in the head inside the blue Passat.

At first the marines wouldn't let us film as their medic patched Zahra up, but relented when we pointed out that they were responsible for shooting her, and it was only because of Mohammed that they had the chance to save her. Our team rescued more injured people, including Zahra's aunt who had a bullet in the shoulder. She could be treated locally, but the marines called in a medevac helicopter to airlift Zahra and her father to Kuwait. All the time, the guys on the wall kept firing. In the hours we spent around the palace that day, they killed five civilians and injured another five. Iraqis – including Mohammed – who had welcomed the Americans were now trembling with fury and outrage.

After a few weeks in hospital in Kuwait, Zahra and her family moved to Iraqi Kurdistan, where it was safer. She survived. The reputation of the Americans did not. The incident we witnessed was one among many. US troops were regarded as liberators for less than twenty-four hours.

The US had been trying to get rid of Saddam Hussein since he invaded Kuwait in 1991. In 1996, the Palestinian-American poet Lisa Suhair Majaj heard a TV interview with the then US Ambassador to the UN, Madeleine Albright. Asked whether the sanctions imposed on Iraq were worth the deaths of half a million Iraqi children, she replied that they were. The poem Suhair Majaj wrote in reaction became even more relevant after the 2003 US invasion, not just because of the 'collateral damage' of civilian deaths but also because the invasion had so many terrible consequences. The world really did 'crack apart'.

Arguments

Lisa Suhair Majaj, 1998

consider the infinite fragility of an infant's skull
how the bones lie soft and open
only time knitting them shut

consider a delicate porcelain bowl –
how it crushes under a single blow
in one moment whole years disappear

consider: beneath the din of explosions
no voice can be heard
no cry

consider your own sky on fire
your name erased
your children's lives 'a price worth paying'

consider the faces you do not see
the eyes you refuse to meet
collateral damage

how in these words
the world
cracks apart

Aleppo, Syria

October 2014

No need for windows – imagine a block of flats with the front sliced off so you can see inside, like an old-fashioned doll's house. Two men in chequered *keffiyeh* head scarves are sitting on a sofa chatting while a little girl in a red dress is dancing. On the level above, a woman in blue is sweeping the floor with rhythmic strokes. A line of washing has been hung across the room. Look a bit closer. The sofa is pushed against some plastic sheeting. Bare concrete pillars hold up the floors and bags of rubble litter the ground. If the little girl dances carelessly she will fall out of the apartment block onto the rough, rain-sodden building site below.

Twenty displaced families were living in that half-built block in the Aleppo suburb of Rouad. We walked up the treacherous open stairs – one misstep could send you tumbling down several flights – to the fourth floor where Mustafa Zakaria Naisa was living with his wife and five children. Rain poured through a crumbling hole in the half-constructed ceiling, and we picked our way through puddles as he showed us the small space they had curtained off for themselves. Peaceful and oblivious, their seven-month-old daughter slept in a cloth they had hung as a hammock.

Mustafa's was the story of Aleppo, a once prosperous city brought to ruin. He had done well as a cobbler, putting away money every month until he had saved enough to buy a small apartment. Then war destroyed his life. Relentless shelling drove the family from their home, and he could no longer make a living.

The only place they could find to stay was the building site. He had done everything he could to protect his children, but to no avail.

Seven-year-old Israa was wearing a red headband with a bow. She should have been starting school that year. Her ten-year-old sister, Kawthar, wore a scarlet T-shirt with the legend 'Girls'. After three years, her education had ceased abruptly. Mustafa looked on with pride as she demonstrated that she could still count to ten in English. 'When I'm grown up I want to be a doctor,' she said. Israa muscled in. She knew numbers too, she said, and insisted on counting to a hundred in Arabic. I didn't ask Mustafa if he thought he would ever be able to send them to school again, because I knew the answer.

The following year, when thousands of Syrian refugees fled to Europe, I found myself looking for Israa and Kawthar. I had no idea if they had fled, and even if they had, I knew that the chances of finding them were minimal, but I couldn't stop looking. There was something about their enthusiasm for learning that made them hard to forget. I thought of my friends' daughters, going through school, on track for university. Geography and history had condemned Kawthar and Israa to early marriage or worse, while in another time and place they might have grown up to be the doctors Kawthar dreamed of. Or mathematicians. Or journalists. I asked a friend visiting Aleppo to see if she could find them, but by the time she located the half-built block, they had moved on, another family displaced time and again by a war that had started as an idealistic revolution.

Siegfried Sassoon's 1939 poem 'The Child at the Window' highlights the innocence of his son, George, and his desire to protect the boy from the war he knew was on its way. Mustafa couldn't protect his daughters – he couldn't even provide a house with a window from which they might look down. They were exposed not only to the elements, but to all the horrors that war can bring.

The Child at the Window

Siegfried Sassoon, 1939

Remember this, when childhood's far away;
The sunlight of a showery first spring day;
You from your house-top window laughing down,
And I, returned with whip-cracks from a ride,
On the great lawn below you, playing the clown.
Time blots our gladness out. Let this with love abide . . .

The brave March day; and you, not four years old,
Up in your nursery world – all heaven for me.
Remember this – the happiness I hold –
In far off springs I shall not live to see;
The world one map of wastening war unrolled,
And you, unconscious of it, setting my spirit free.

For you must learn, beyond bewildering years,
How little things beloved and held are best.
The windows of the world are blurred with tears,
And troubles come like cloud-banks from the west.
Remember this, some afternoon in spring,
When your own child looks down and makes your sad
    heart sing.

Ingushetia, Russia

November 1999

'Beslan Itsarayev will not survive,' I wrote in the *Observer*. 'His gaunt face has the pale, waxen look of an old man on the verge of death. He is thirteen years old. His eyes roll up in their sockets and his wasted body is skeletal.'

We were at Slephsozsk Hospital, a few miles from the border with Chechnya. Three months earlier, Russia had mounted first a massive aerial bombardment on the breakaway republic and then a ground invasion. Sometimes the Russian soldiers who guarded the border with Ingushetia allowed injured civilians to cross, and sometimes not. Beslan had been walking home from the market in the town of Urus-Martan when Russian bombers attacked. He was hit in the stomach. Unable to absorb food and needing surgery, he spent a month being shunted from hospital to hospital in Chechnya and had only been allowed across the border a few days earlier.

'When the wounded come straight from the battlefield it's easier to treat them,' said the surgeon, Dr Tamara Malsakova, neat in her white coat and tall white hat. 'Maybe if this boy had come here directly, he wouldn't be in this critical state.'

Beslan's mother, Hijan, didn't have the US$40 needed to buy her son's medicine. It seemed hopeless, but we gave her the money, finished our filming and moved on. In the weeks that followed, however, I found I couldn't 'move on'. I couldn't get Beslan Itsarayev out of my mind. I felt that by predicting his death in print I had in some way condemned him. Rationally, I knew his plight wasn't my fault, but I felt guilty nonetheless.

A few months later, I was back in Ingushetia reporting on the refugees pouring out of Chechnya. It was colder and even more miserable. We happened to pass the hospital, so I dropped in to check what had happened. As I approached, a plump woman in a flowered headscarf rushed up, threw her arms around me and started crying. It was Hijan. Beslan was much better, she said. The US$40 medicine had worked. She took me to see him in the ward. There was now flesh on his bones. He could take food. He smiled. I have never been so happy to get a story wrong. Beslan Itsarayev would survive.

Fiona Benson's poem 'Eurofighter Typhoon' brings home the terror of an air raid like the one in which Beslan was injured. It does what we as journalists often fail to do – makes you feel what it would be like if it were your child.

Fiona Benson

Eurofighter Typhoon, 2019

My daughters are playing outside with plastic hoops;
the elder is trying to hula, over and over –
it falls off her hips, but she keeps trying,
and the younger is watching and giggling,
and they're happy in the bright afternoon.
I'm indoors at the hob with the door open
so I can see them, because the elder might trip,
and the younger is still a baby and liable to eat dirt,
when out of clear skies a jet comes in low
over the village. At the first muted roar
the elder runs in squealing then stops in the kitchen,
her eyes adjusting to the dimness, looking foolish
and unsure. I drop the spoon and bag of peas
and leave her frightened and tittering, wiping my hands
on my jeans, trying to walk and not run,
because I don't want to scare the baby
who's still sat on the patio alone, looking for her sister,
bewildered, trying to figure why she's gone –
all this in the odd, dead pause of the lag –
then sound catches up with the plane
and now its grey belly's right over our house
with a metallic, grinding scream
like the sky's being chainsawed open
and the baby's face drops to a square of pure fear,

she tips forward and flattens her body on the ground
and presses her face into the concrete slab.
I scoop her up and she presses in shuddering,
screaming her strange, halt pain cry
and it's all right now I tell her again and again,
but it's never all right now – Christ have mercy –
my daughter in my arms can't steady me –
always some woman is running to catch up her children,
we dig them out of the rubble in parts like plaster dolls –
Mary Mother of God have mercy, mercy on us all.

Kibilizi, Rwanda

April 2014

The children born of rape during Rwanda's 1994 genocide are adults now. In Kibilizi, near Butare, twelve of them grew up with their mothers at one end of the village. Their fathers lived at the other end. A hostile silence hovered over the red dirt road between, sometimes interrupted in the night when the men's relatives would throw stones at the women's houses. Some of the men had been *Interahamwe*, members of the cruel Hutu militia that had murdered hundreds of thousands of Rwanda's Tutsis. The women and children – most of whose other relatives had been killed in the genocide – lived in fear and poverty, but they had nowhere else to go.

In Rwandan custom, a child is given a Christian and a Kinyarwanda name. Epiphane Mukamakombe, who made several attempts to abort, called her son Olivier Utabazi, meaning 'he belongs to them'. She refused to breastfeed and tried to kill him when he was a baby. 'I used to hit him and the house was full of sticks. I didn't even want to talk to him. When he was still little, about seven years old, I beat him a lot. I didn't love him. I felt he was an *Interahamwe*,' she told me. Unsurprisingly, he was a sullen and aggressive child.

By the time I met him, Olivier was nineteen. His defiant stare softened when he tried to explain the complexity and pain of his circumstance. He could understand why his mother was cruel to him, but he couldn't bring himself to hate his father. 'On the one hand I blame my father because he raped my mother and didn't help her bring me up,' he said. 'But on the other hand, I don't know if he was really a bad man. Maybe they were going to kill my mother and then my father told her, if you let us have sex with you, we won't kill you, so mum had to agree.' Such was the logic of genocide.

A therapist, Marie Josée Ukeye, helped the women and children overcome the pain and stigma they felt. 'The adolescent girls are ashamed and often take on the suffering of their mothers, while the boys have explosive fits of temper,' she said. Over time, Epiphane began to see her son in a different light. 'The love came later when I realised God gave this child to me and he's the only family I have,' she said. 'I cannot blame him for how he was born.' Olivier just wanted to get away, to go to Kigali or another place where people wouldn't know who he was or how he had been conceived. Yet he felt responsible for his mother.

After my visit, Olivier kept trying to contact me on Facebook. Marie Josée advised me not to respond, because it would give him unwarranted hope that I could solve his problems. Nonetheless, a few years later he managed to get a message through: he had made it to university in Kigali to study engineering. He was on course to earn enough money to support his mother. It was, I thought, quite an achievement – it's hard to imagine a child born in more dreadful circumstances, and yet he had in some ways overcome his heritage.

Warsan Shire – a British-Somali poet born in Kenya – reflects on the danger of sexual assault that women face in war, the terrifying intimacy of such violence and the shadow that hangs over the children of rape.

Your Mother's First Kiss

Warsan Shire, 2011

The first boy to kiss your mother later raped women
when the war broke out. She remembers hearing this
from your uncle, then going to your bedroom and laying
down on the floor. You were at school.

Your mother was sixteen when he first kissed her.
She held her breath for so long that she blacked out.
On waking she found her dress was wet and sticking
to her stomach, half moons bitten into her thighs.

That same evening she visited a friend, a girl
who fermented wine illegally in her bedroom.
When your mother confessed I've never been touched
like that before, the friend laughed, mouth bloody with grapes,
then plunged a hand between your mother's legs.

Last week, she saw him driving the number 18 bus,
his cheek a swollen drumlin, a vine scar dragging itself
across his mouth. You were with her, holding a bag
of dates to your chest, heard her let out a deep moan
when she saw how much you looked like him.

Beslan, Russia

September 2004

The sky darkened and rain came down in torrents as the people of Beslan buried their children in a field on the edge of town. Earth-moving machines were digging yet more graves. The mourners seemed oblivious to the television cameras: they were too deep in sorrow. Some coffins remained open in the Orthodox Christian tradition. I turned away as a middle-aged woman in glasses, her tears mingling with the rain, leant over the grave to kiss her son for the last time. He looked about eight. It was unspeakable. 'You were always on time,' sobbed another. 'Why couldn't you be late that day?' We stopped filming. It was too much.

A week earlier, the parents had taken their children to Beslan School Number One for the beginning of the academic year, celebrated as Knowledge Day across Russia. They came with traditional gifts and flowers for the teachers, but celebration soon turned to horror. At 9am, armed men and women, masked and wearing suicide belts, took over the school and held hostage those who did not manage to flee. They had been sent by the Chechen warlord Shamil Basayev who was demanding independence for Chechnya and had orchestrated similar hostage-taking at the Dubrovka Theatre in Moscow two years earlier. That had ended in disaster after Russian forces pumped gas which not only killed the hostage-takers but many of the hostages too.

The temperature inside the school rose, and some children

died of dehydration because the hostage-takers denied them water. Some adults were executed. The hostages were held in the school gymnasium, which had been rigged with explosive devices. As news spread, various branches of local and national government sent in competing security forces. No one was in overall command. Soldiers, some in tanks, armed with rockets, grenade launchers, flamethrowers and other weapons stood behind local men carrying ancient hunting rifles. They established no proper perimeter, none of the basic measures any security force would impose in a hostage situation.

The Russian government, under its new prime minister, Vladimir Putin, refused several opportunities for negotiation. They wanted to look tough, and their actions showed that they had no regard for the lives of the hostages. On the third day, two explosions sounded. Instead of waiting to see what had happened, the security forces opened up with all their weapons. The roof of the school went up in flames, and hostages including children ran out into the gunfire. Some of the uncles and fathers in the front line may have killed their own children in the chaos. More than 300 hostages were killed, at least 185 of them children. The following day, instead of carefully guarding the crime scene, Russian officials sent bulldozers to destroy it. They obstructed inquiries, covering up their own culpability.

The Irish poet Eavan Boland wrote 'Child of Our Time' during the Troubles in Northern Ireland. In May 1974, violence came south across the border and a series of car bombs were detonated in Dublin and Monaghan, killing thirty-four people including two small children. Responsibility, as she saw it, lay not just with the bombers but with all who failed to protect the victims, especially the children.

Child of Our Time

Eavan Boland, 1975

Yesterday I knew no lullaby
But you have taught me overnight to order
This song, which takes from your final cry
Its tune, from your unreasoned end its reason;
Its rhythm from the discord of your murder,
Its motive from the fact you cannot listen.

We who should have known how to instruct
With rhymes for your waking, rhythms for your sleep,
Names for the animals you took to bed,
Tales to distract, legends to protect,
Later an idiom for you to keep
And living, learn, must learn from you, dead,

To make our broken images rebuild
Themselves around your limbs, your broken
Image, find for your sake whose life our idle
Talk has cost, a new language. Child
Of our time, our times have robbed your cradle.
Sleep in a world your final sleep has woken.

WARLORDS

Perfection, of a kind, was what he was after

Some dictators and warlords I have met were terrifying, others dangerously charming, and a few were both. Dictators are more likely than democrats to start wars, either by using force to suppress rebels and minorities within their own country, or by invading a neighbour. (The US and UK invaded Iraq and Afghanistan, but democracies rarely go to war with each other.) War sustains dictatorship, because under martial law opposition can be more easily suppressed. Warlords who seize territory suddenly find that they have power and wealth that can only be maintained by continuing or expanding the conflict. Absolute power doesn't only corrupt, it drives leaders mad, as they use ever more extreme forms of violence to retain their own position.

Pale, Republika Srpska, Bosnia

June 1996

Radovan Karadžić didn't give the impression of a man on the run. He strode confidently into his large, carpeted office, sat down at a mahogany table and offered me wild strawberries from a bowl in the centre. 'So much harder to pick now because of the land-mines,' he remarked. A well-built young man with a pistol tucked into his jeans pocket prowled the room.

Karadžić was wanted by the International Criminal Tribunal for the former Yugoslavia (ICTY) for ethnic cleansing, ordering death camps of Bosnian Muslims and Croats, and masterminding the siege of Sarajevo when he had been president of the Serb statelet of Republika Srpska during the Bosnian War. He wasn't difficult to find, but the international peacekeeping troops we passed every day didn't seem to be looking very hard. We had run into the current president of Srpska, Biljana Plavšić, at the cemetery the day before and asked if we could meet the man we knew was still really her boss. She had told us to come to a disused factory on the edge of town at 2.30pm the following day. He was in the office adjacent to hers.

With his sweeping mane of grey hair and urbane manner, Karadžić loved the limelight. He smoked Cuban cigars, drank French cognac and had been a psychiatrist and a poet before the war. Under the terms of the Dayton Peace Accords which had brought the conflict to an end six months earlier, he was official-ly barred from giving interviews, so he wouldn't let us film. The previous year he had ordered the Bosnian Serb military to massacre 7,000 men and boys at Srebrenica – the defining atrocity of the Bosnian conflict. Now he wanted to show us his plans for turning the red-roofed village of Pale, where his support was strongest, into the Hong Kong of the Balkans. The walls of his office were plastered with maps, which he jabbed at with a pointer that he pulled from his pocket.

He indicated an area in pink. 'This is where we'll have our Wall Street,' he explained. 'There'll be a stock market, two hotels and a banking area. Blue is the residential area and yellow, industrial.' Other maps showed plans for an oil refinery, a power station and 150 miles of roads and railways. His fiefdom, I thought, was more like Mervyn Peake's fantasy kingdom of Gormenghast than Hong Kong. This was a ferociously delusional display of hubris.

Karadžić vanished a few months later – mine was amongst the last interviews he gave. A volume of apparently execrable poetry – entitled, bafflingly, *Under the Left Breast of the Century* – was produced while in hiding. (I will spare readers, apart from noting that he referred to his enemies as 'you vial of scum, you vial of snails'.) Then, in 2008, a New Age faith healer going by the name of Dragan David Dabic was arrested in Belgrade. It was Karadžić. Sporting a long, white beard, his hair tied in a top-knot with a black ribbon and wearing thick glasses, he had gone unrecognised for more than a decade. In 2016, he was convicted of genocide, crimes against humanity and war crimes. He's serving his life sentence in a prison somewhere in the UK.

W. H. Auden's 'Epitaph on a Tyrant' fits Karadžić closely. His Hong Kong fantasies were a form of perfection for his Serb nationalist dream. He even wrote bad poetry. And his acolytes laughed obediently, while the people of Bosnia died in their thousands.

Epitaph on a Tyrant

W. H. Auden, 1939

Perfection, of a kind, was what he was after,
And the poetry he invented was easy to understand;
He knew human folly like the back of his hand,
And was greatly interested in armies and fleets;
When he laughed, respectable senators burst with laughter,
And when he cried the little children died in the streets.

Baghdad, Iraq

October 2002

'Every joke is a tiny revolution,' said George Orwell. Dictators do not have a sense of humour, so laughter is the only way those who live under dictatorship survive. No ruler was more feared than Saddam Hussein, who had personally shot several of his opponents and ordered Kurdish civilians to be gassed. I was surprised then to find out that the most popular play in Baghdad in 2002, the year before he was ousted in the US-led invasion, was a satire on the corruption of the regime. *Don't Tell Me, I've Seen it for Myself* played to packed houses for four years before war brought the run to an abrupt end.

The night I went, the Nasr Theatre was buzzing. Plastic chairs were crammed in to accommodate latecomers, blocking the aisles. I have never seen an audience laugh so uproariously. As they made their entrance, the male and female leads were greeted with wolf-whistles and applause. He was tall, dark and handsome. She was a pneumatic blonde in a slinky black dress with a scarlet feather boa and a slash of crimson lipstick. Speaking no Arabic, my understanding was limited, but I think the plot went as follows. An unlikely group of stock characters, including a drunk, a dwarf and a good-for-nothing, live in a place not unlike Baghdad under sanctions. They are taken hostage and transported to Mars. (At this point the dwarf appeared in a shining silver suit, with an inverted red plastic bucket on his head.) Then there's a nuclear war.

The female lead was apparently well-known in real life for her close relations with senior government officials, liaisons that cushioned her from the hardship of life. The drunk reads her palm. 'I see something that goes for six hours and comes for three...'

The audience, weary of persistent power cuts, yells 'ELECTRICITY!'

'Oh, really?' she says.

'Well, you wouldn't know,' says the drunk. 'You just phone one of your friends and the lights come on!'

'It tells us everything about our lives,' said a woman in a red brocade dress, her heavy eye make-up running from tears of mirth. 'It's the real situation in Iraq,' explained her friend, who was in full chador. A young man told me he had seen it seven times.

There were jokes about the children of the Ba'ath Party elite cheating at school, and the need for a bribe to get a government official to perform the smallest bureaucratic service. Ministers were mocked mercilessly, but there were no jokes directed at Saddam and his family – that was off limits. In a dictatorship, writers and artists have to tread a careful line.

The Myanmar poet Maung Saungkha stepped over it in 2016 with his short poem 'Image' about President Thein Sein, which he published on Facebook. He went on the run when he heard he was to be arrested. 'You can arrest only the poets, not the poems,' he wrote while in hiding. He was eventually convicted of defamation and sentenced to six months in prison. He now commands a guerilla army, fighting the generals – including the one he insulted – who run Myanmar.

Image

Maung Saungkha, 2016

I have the President's portrait tattooed on my penis
How disgusted my wife is.

Khartoum, Sudan

1989 and 2008

The first time I met Brigadier-General Omar al-Bashir, he had just led the coup that ousted the democratically elected government of Sudan. His inexperience as a military dictator was matched by mine as a journalist – neither of us knew how to bring our interview to an end. Eventually, as my questions grew more nebulous, he got up from behind his desk, walked across his office, turned on the TV, sat down and began to watch *Tom and Jerry*. My audience with Sudan's new leader was over.

In contrast to flamboyant characters like Karadžić, Gaddafi or Saddam Hussein, al-Bashir was a small, bald, utterly forgettable man. I expected him to last a few months before a more charismatic figure took over. How wrong I was. By allying with the Islamists and perfecting the art of juggling factions and personalities, he would manage to remain in power for three decades. Under the rule of al-Bashir, the army consolidated its hold on the country's economy, while outsourcing much of the fighting in Sudan's multiple civil wars to locally recruited militia. When African rebels in the western region of Darfur started an armed insurgency in the early 2000s, al-Bashir created an Arab militia called the *Janjaweed* – devils on horseback – to put down the rebellion. Their cruelty was terrifying. I saw the villages they burnt and talked to some of the women they raped.

In 2008, the prosecutor of the International Criminal Court charged Omar al-Bashir with genocide, war crimes and crimes against humanity for the campaign in Darfur. I flew to Khartoum to interview him again. This time he was surrounded by flunkies, but the decades in power had not enhanced his charisma. He was a bureaucrat of terror. Like Adolf Eichmann, the Nazi official Hannah Arendt described as 'terrifyingly normal', his evil was distinctly banal. He simply denied all the charges against him. 'Everything is fabricated and made up,' he said. 'Anything saying that we ordered killing people is untrue.'

When I confronted him with a dossier detailing mass rape, he smiled. 'We are fully convinced that no rape took place. There are scientific methods that can reveal who are the fathers of these children which are born.' But the rapists operated in gangs, and the women didn't know the identity of the individuals. Was he really planning to take the DNA of all the *Janjaweed*? 'Mass rape does not exist,' he replied, his eyes darting like a lizard's. 'The Darfurian society does not have rape.'

Twenty years later, after he was ousted, his creature, the *Janjaweed*, now called the Rapid Support Forces, turned against the army. It was a case of Frankenstein's monster, except Frankenstein was now in retirement. The RSF restarted the *Janjaweed* campaign of terror against Africans in Darfur. In 2024, I interviewed refugees fleeing across the border to Chad and heard exactly the same stories of murder, looting and rape that I had heard in 2003. In Omdurman, Khartoum's twin city, I saw a house the RSF had used a torture chamber – they had rigged up a pulley system to hoist their victims over a pit dug in the floor. Al-Bashir might have gone, I thought, but his cruel legacy survives.

The German playwright and poet Bertolt Brecht had a masterful eye for the absurdity of war and the duplicitous language a dictator will use to maintain power. A lifelong pacifist, he wrote in protest against fascism and war throughout his career and fled Nazi Germany in 1939. His personification of 'The God of War' as a cruel figure who wants to take up very little of his audience's time, conjures the unassuming al-Bashir.

The God of War

Bertolt Brecht, 1938
Translated from the German by
Michael Hamburger

I saw the old god of war stand in a bog between chasm and
    rockface.

He smelled of free beer and carbolic and showed his testicles
    to adolescents, for he had been rejuvenated by several
    professors. In a hoarse wolfish voice he declared his love
    for everything young. Nearby stood a pregnant woman,
    trembling.

And without shame he talked on and presented himself as
    a great one for order. And he described how everywhere
    he put barns in order, by emptying them.

And as one throws crumbs to sparrows, he fed poor people
    with crusts of bread which he had taken away from
    poor people.

His voice was now loud, now soft, but always hoarse.

In a loud voice he spoke of great times to come, and in a soft
    voice he taught the women how to cook crows and seagulls.

Meanwhile his back was unquiet, and he kept looking round, as though afraid of being stabbed.

And every five minutes he assured his public that he would take up very little of their time.

Ethiopian/Eritrean border

May 1998

This is how the war started. Two bald men squabbling over a comb.

For decades Meles Zenawi and Isaias Afwerki fought alongside each other to overthrow the Ethiopian communist government of Mengistu Haile Mariam. After their victory in 1991, they agreed that Eritrea – which had been annexed by Ethiopia in 1962 – should secede. Zenawi became the Ethiopian president, Afwerki the first president of an independent Eritrea. Less than a decade later the two countries were at war over a line on a map.

The impoverished peasant farmers who lived around the small town of Badme, tending livestock on the sparse, parched earth, were not consulted about the location of the border. According to old colonial maps, Badme was in Eritrea. However, it was administered as part of the Ethiopian province of Tigray, which didn't really matter as long as Eritrea was also part of Ethiopia. One day in May 1998 – five years after Eritrean independence – Ethiopian police arrived to demarcate a new international border that had Badme on the Ethiopian side. The Eritreans responded by sending soldiers to claim the land.

I went to Addis Ababa to interview Zenawi, smart in his dark suit and tie, projecting the image of a responsible head of state. He was a short man with a shiny face and a small, precise moustache, much celebrated at the time by optimistic western leaders such as Tony Blair hoping for an 'African Renaissance' of democracy.

'If every African leader were to wake up some morning and decide it's time to bite off a chunk of this territory or that territory, and get away with it, we'd have the law of the jungle,' Zenawi said, blaming Afwerki for starting the war. Surely old comrades-at-arms could negotiate? 'There isn't much left of that friendship,' he said, coldly. 'We don't have to be friends to live together. We are neighbours.'

A few days later I made it to the Eritrean capital, Asmara, to meet Afwerki, tall and lanky, dressed in khaki, with a much bushier moustache. I was with a journalist who knew him from his days fighting in the bush; on her advice we brought him a cassette of his favourite band, The Pogues, who played Irish folk-punk. In contrast to Zenawi, the sober statesman, he presented himself as the evergreen rebel leader, but he had the same explanation for the war: his former friend had grabbed his country's land. 'Had that been in the law, the rule of the game, Africa would be in a perpetual war and all those with the might would have the right to invade,' he said. And the friendship? 'At the moment these emotions are put aside.'

In the months that followed, thousands of Ethiopians were expelled from Eritrea, and Eritreans from Ethiopia. After two years, the leaders agreed to mediation. By then, at least 70,000 people were dead, millions displaced, and billions of dollars had been spent on armaments. A final resolution to the border dispute took twenty years.

After the war, Meles Zenawi became more autocratic, locking up his perceived rivals until his death in 2012. Afwerki put his country on a perpetual war footing. Young Eritreans – men and women – are still required to perform indefinite military service. He has cut Eritrea off from the world, like an African North Korea. Academic studies have analysed the underlying causes of the conflict: economic friction, ethnic tension, the perpetual problems caused by colonial boundaries. But fundamentally it was caused by the stubbornness of two men for whom war had become a way of life, and who saw negotiation and compromise as a form of weakness.

The South African poet Len Verwey, who was born in Mozambique, grew up with violence and war. His poem 'Campaign' looks at a war over maps from the point of view of fighters who lose their humanity carrying out the orders of leaders who sleep soundly in their beds.

Campaign

Len Verwey, 2014

We set off and return in grayness, pass
the growing animal entourage that
sleeps curled against the perimeter wire,
close as it can manage to our fires.

The severed heads poled along the highway:
a leering puppetry
fitted to the dim-dawned place we've made.
Only the very old and very young
in the villages we raze.

Our generals sleep soundly, without exception,
wake slowly
to their coffee in the morning.

Nights I have stood outside my tent, seen
the orange glow far across the dark space
ringing the plateau, yet felt the heat on my skin,
felt that I could fan the flames from
where I stood, if I wanted.

All around me, not only in the directions where I knew
the villages lay, this glow
like a candle's light on the inside of a tent.

I concluded nothing then.
To think too far along such lines,
while others sleep, is to risk everything.

We torched the maps
when we torched the crops.
We torched the crops
when we knew those back home
wouldn't take us in again.

The maps meant nothing anyway.

Abbottabad, Pakistan

May 2011

On my desk at home I have a small, hinged chunk of dark metal with a broken spring, part of a US stealth helicopter that crashed in the operation to kill Osama bin Laden. I bought it for a few rupees from one of the kids hawking souvenirs outside the fortified compound in Abbottabad, Pakistan, where the al-Qaeda leader had lived in hiding and met his end at the hands of US Navy Seals.

A decade earlier, on bin Laden's orders, jihadis had blown up the Twin Towers in New York and changed the world. Now, curious Pakistanis had come to look at the place where – unbeknownst to them – the al-Qaeda leader had been living undisturbed for five years. Pakistani soldiers would not let them – or us – enter. A five-metre-high outer wall topped with barbed wire surrounded the compound which contained the three-storey villa where the FBI's most wanted terrorist and his family had lived. Through the gate we could glimpse a two-metre-high inner wall. It was a fortress.

The children were eager to talk. 'I used to go to their house,' boasted twelve-year-old Zarar Ahmed. 'He had two wives. I saw three children, a girl and two boys. They gave me two rabbits.' Had nothing raised their suspicions? Apart from the lucky recipient of the rabbits, even children had been barred from entry. 'Whenever the local children's ball went into that compound, they would knock on the door, and those people would tell them, there's no ball here, and give them money,' explained a teacher. 'Their own children didn't play outside.' The children from the compound did, however, sometimes go to the corner shop to buy sodas and sweets in the company of the two brothers who had looked after the bin Laden family. The only other people who entered the compound were health workers administering polio vaccinations. (Later we learnt they had been employed by the CIA – a reckless move that discredited vaccination in the eyes of many Afghans and Pakistanis.)

Someone had painted an advertisement for a girls' school on the outer wall. There was irony, I thought, in how this man who believed that women should be hidden from the world had ended up in a kind of purdah himself. Locals had thought that a drug dealer or smuggler must live inside, although it seemed scarcely credible that Pakistani intelligence – much of which was sympathetic to al-Qaeda – didn't know the identity of a man who lived in such ostentatious seclusion in a garrison town.

The Americans didn't notify the Pakistani authorities before launching their raid. Bin Laden and several of the men were shot dead, while the women and children were captured. His death marked the end of one stage of what the Americans called the Global War on Terror.

It was strange to think that a man who had attacked the heart of American power, and loomed so large in the world's imagination, was gone. His destructive, cruel interpretation of Islam lived on, morphing into an even more extreme version under the Islamic State. But the man himself was dead, his body about to be cast into the sea so a burial place could never become a shrine – and nor could his compound, which the Pakistani government destroyed the following year.

In 2017, the CIA released a cache of computer files recovered from the house, including a video of bin Laden's son's wedding, the animated films *Chicken Little* and *Ice Age: Dawn of the*

Dinosaurs, and a digitised version of a handwritten diary in which bin Laden expressed the hope that the Arab Spring revolts would usher in Islamist rule. There was no evidence that he still controlled jihadi warriors from the villa – his power had already ebbed away. Digital traces don't have the romance of the stone fragments of Shelley's ancient king, whose achievements were lost in the vast desert of time stretching into infinity. But the banal debris of bin Laden's life still serve as a reminder that even the most powerful and terrifying dictators and warlords eventually meet their fate.

Ozymandias

Percy Bysshe Shelley, 1817

I met a traveller from an antique land,
Who said—'Two vast and trunkless legs of stone
Stand in the desert . . . Near them, on the sand,
Half sunk a shattered visage lies, whose frown,
And wrinkled lip, and sneer of cold command,
Tell that its sculptor well those passions read
Which yet survive, stamped on these lifeless things,
The hand that mocked them, and the heart that fed;
And on the pedestal, these words appear:
My name is Ozymandias, King of Kings;
Look on my Works, ye Mighty, and despair!
Nothing beside remains. Round the decay
Of that colossal Wreck, boundless and bare
The lone and level sands stretch far away.'

REFUGEES

Like chaff we were borne in the wind

People have fled conflict and natural disaster since history began – if they hadn't, the human race would have died out long ago. The distinction between political persecution and economic migration isn't always clear-cut: many of the refugees I've met are escaping a complex mixture of problems that may defy a simple explanation to a border guard or immigration official. Being a refugee is never easy, especially in countries where you're made to feel unwelcome. While European electorates often resent the arrival of just a few thousand refugees, many much poorer countries take in millions. According to the office of the UN High Commissioner for Refugees, by May 2024, 120 million people worldwide – the largest numbers from Sudan, Syria, Ukraine and Afghanistan – were defined as 'forcibly displaced', having fled conflict, human rights abuse and the impact of climate change. Some had remained within their own countries, while others crossed a border. The civil wars in Sudan and Gaza were the most acute crises, creating more refugees daily, but there was competition from Myanmar and the Democratic Republic of Congo. The top five countries hosting refugees were Turkey, Iran, Colombia (owing to the economic crisis in Venezuela), Germany and Pakistan.

Europe

The summer of 2015

It was the summer of hope. I travelled with refugees by ferry, train and foot from Greece through Macedonia, Serbia and Hungary to Austria. They had come from Syria, Iraq, Iran, Afghanistan, Bangladesh, Nigeria, Mali and a dozen other countries, fleeing war, poverty and despair. They carried backpacks and sleeping bags, manoeuvring wheelchairs and pushchairs across fields, gangplanks and railway platforms. It was the summer that Angela Merkel, the German chancellor, agreed that a million refugees could settle in Germany and Viktor Orbán, the Hungarian prime minister, built a barbed wire fence to keep them out.

My notebooks are full of fragments of stories from Aleppo, Suleimaniya and Kabul, but what remains in my memory are images. A little girl with curly dark hair knelt on the small table jutting into the carriage from a train window, watching rapt as the unfamiliar landscape sped by. The rest of her family was slumped across the seats, exhausted from the arduous journey through Turkey and Greece, but she was enthralled by the new world opening up before her. A small Syrian boy smiled as he brandished a plastic brontosaurus while his family waited on the border between Hungary and Austria. Any fear or weariness he might have felt had been extinguished by this wondrous new possession, the gift of an Austrian volunteer. A toddler wriggled in a luggage cart at Vienna station while his parents, who spoke and read no German, tried to work out which was the train to Frankfurt.

The children stay in my mind because I knew that this was the defining moment of their lives but they did not. Later, they would understand the significance of that summer, and the arbitrariness of fate which meant they would become German, while their friends back home would grow up in the old life, or worse, perish. I was witnessing a moment in the millennia James Fenton evokes in his poem 'Wind'; as families were divided, new languages learnt and old ones forgotten, and decisions made in haste would change the fate of generations to come.

Wind

James Fenton, 1982

This is the wind, the wind in a field of corn.
Great crowds are fleeing from a major disaster
Down the long valleys, the green swaying wadis,
Down through the beautiful catastrophe of wind.

Families, tribes, nations and their livestock
Have heard something, seen something. An expectation
Or a gigantic misunderstanding has swept over the hilltop
Bending the ear of the hedgerow with stories of fire and sword.

I saw a thousand years pass in two seconds.
Land was lost, languages rose and divided.
The lord went east and found safety.
His brother sought Africa and a dish of aloes.

Centuries, minutes later, one might ask
How the hilt of a sword wandered so far from the smithy.
And somewhere they will sing: 'Like chaff we were borne
In the wind.' This is the wind in a field of corn.

Kabul, Afghanistan and Vestnes, Norway

May 2021–December 2022

Farzana Kochi's parents made sure she got an education despite the edicts of the Taliban and the war that formed the backdrop to her childhood. She grew up determined to help her nomadic Kochi community, especially the women. In 2018, aged twenty-six, she was elected as a member of the Afghan parliament.

On a barren hillside outside Kabul, I watched her talk to a group of constituents in a ragged seasonal camp. Taking notes about the people's needs – better tents, education for the children – she commanded the respect of not only the women but also the men. 'We have ten Kochi MPs and she's the only one who visited us,' said one elder. 'She's like our daughter. Why wouldn't we vote for her?' The Taliban and the even more extreme Islamic State–Khorasan Province (IS–K) thought differently. The writ of the US-backed government didn't extend far beyond the city limits, and Farzana had received death threats. We didn't stay long at the camp. Her security guards hustled her away.

Farzana was unusual amongst Afghan women, remaining unmarried into her late twenties and being the main breadwinner for her extended family. After the Taliban returned to power in August 2021, she wanted to stay in Afghanistan, not least because she was responsible for her elderly mother and the children of her sister, who was separated from her husband. As the Taliban consolidated control, each day became more difficult.

'I'm lost totally,' she messaged me by WhatsApp. 'They just said that no women anymore.'

Determined to speak up for Afghan women, she continued to talk to the media, although that raised her profile. 'Searching for a place to hide while we aren't safe,' she messaged. 'From Taliban to IS-K to US drone all make us feel unsafe. I don't know where to go.'

She had been offered asylum in Norway but it was impossible to get all her extended family accepted. She didn't want to go without her mother and dependent nephews and nieces, but when armed men raided her office while she was out, she knew it was only a matter of time before they found her. She sent me a picture of herself dressed not in the brightly coloured traditional Kochi clothes she usually wore, but in a black niqab, with only her eyes showing. It was the disguise that she had used to escape with her brother as *mahram*, the male guardian on which the Taliban insisted. Weeks of complex arrangements followed. By the time her mother and brothers were granted asylum in Canada, Farzana, with her brother, sister and her sister's children, were already in a fishing town on the north-west coast of Norway. She was torn between trying to start a new life, feeling guilty about not being with her mother and worrying about what was happening back home.

'I feel responsible for people in Afghanistan struggling with Taliban. People are suffering silently,' she wrote. Eventually, Farzana managed to visit her mother in Canada, where she hopes that eventually she'll be allowed to settle, but she cannot stop thinking about the women of Afghanistan she has left behind who are facing ever more restrictions. She messaged me: 'How difficult it is to be a woman in this world.'

Like all stories, Farzana's is unique, but it's recognisable to thousands of other women forced into exile. Warsan Shire writes of a refugee who also feels responsible for her mother, and who cannot shake off the nightmares or rid herself of the stench of war.

War Poem (*extract*)

Warsan Shire, 2017

1.

There is a war going on in my country. In all the years I have
lived in this body, there has been no peace. My mother still
has hope in her heart, she keeps a suitcase packed just in
case. This whole life we have been waiting for our flight to be
called. In the recurring dream I board a plane to Mogadishu.
Every passenger on the plane is my mother, my mother in
the seat beside me reading a crime novel, my mother in an
ill-fitting uniform serving drinks, my mother as the pilot,
winking, tipping his cap. When the plane starts to fall out
the sky I wake up.

2.

Look, one war giving birth to another
one war crawling out from between the
legs of another, out of the rubble
of one war crawls out another
look, a snake swallowing its own head.

3.

What do I do? I think I brought the war with me
unknowingly, perhaps on my skin, plumes
of it in my hair, under my nails. It sits with me,
watches my favourite TV shows,

sighs in the pauses of telephone calls,
sleeps between me and my partner in bed,
stands behind me in the shower – lathers my back,
presses the pill into my night time tongue,
at the bathroom sink uses its blue hand to
touch my cheek.

Even the dentist jumped back from the wormhole
of my mouth, I suspect it was probably the war
he saw. What do I do? I want to make love but my hair
smells of war and running and running.

Misrata, Libya

April 2015

Every few days, the tide would bring back bodies to the Libyan shore. They were washed and shrouded at the Misrata mosque before being buried in a makeshift cemetery amongst the dunes overlooking the Mediterranean. I counted thirty-seven fresh graves, anonymous men and women lying near the beach from which they had set sail. I looked out to sea as they must have done, towards Europe, the land of their dreams and aspirations.

Refugees and migrants have long taken boats from along the coast of Libya, but in the spring and summer of 2015, as the central government in Libya collapsed and militia took over fragmented territories, smugglers seized their opportunity. Sabratha, west of Tripoli, and Misrata, to the east, were the main ports of exit. For a sum, smugglers would put refugees on small boats and equip them with a phone so when they reached Italian waters, they could call the Italian coastguard who would be obliged to rescue them. Often, the boats would start to sink while in Libyan waters, or the Italians would say they were in Libyan waters to avoid responsibility. The unsuccessful would drown or be forced back to Libya and imprisoned.

Some of those who took to the boats were Syrians fleeing war, but most were African men who had trekked across the desert to the coast in search of a life above the bare minimum of survival back home. As I stood outside the Misrata detention centre, men pushed notes through the bars with the phone numbers of families in Ibadan, Banjul and Ouagadougou whom they wanted me to call. Five hundred and sixty men had been detained after being stopped at sea. Wisdom, whose boat had been intercepted a few weeks earlier, told me that he had been put in charge of navigation. 'I drew the map of Africa and Europe, and I put a compass at the centre, pointing forwards,' he said. 'We were clapping and singing, but then we heard a big horn from the rear. It was the Libyan coastguard. They brought us here.'

Eritreans were the largest group in the detention centre. If they'd stayed at home they would have been forced into indefinite military service. An earnest young man named Yonatan told me that his brother had been in the Eritrean army for twenty years. He showed me the things he had carried on his odyssey, including a Bible he kept concealed in a grubby cloth. 'You can touch it, but don't let the guards see it,' he said. He feared that the Muslims who ran the detention centre would confiscate it.

Wisdom ended up back home in Nigeria. Yonatan took another boat and made it to Sweden where he had family. But that year, more than 5,000 migrants drowned in the Mediterranean. Who was to blame? The European governments who refused to rescue them? The smugglers? The African governments who failed to provide a living for their citizens? Or the migrants themselves who had decided to try their luck in the hope of a better life?

The Libyan-American poet Khaled Mattawa wrote about someone no journalist had thought to interview: the wife of a man who sells boats to the smugglers, another person in the chain of profit on land and loss at sea.

The Boat Merchant's Wife

Khaled Mattawa, 2019

Sabratha

He started out making feluccas;
an Egyptian taught him how.
Then he opened a shop by the beach,

sold ice cream, parasols and chairs.
He asked for my hand when I was
in teacher college, first year.

Time passes like the Ghibli* here.
I was 7 months with my third baby
when someone sought him

for a Zodiac. He traveled all the way
to Guangzhou, brought back a dozen,
has been selling them ever since.

One night I asked how strong
they were, how many they carry.
'It's all in the booklet,' he said,

* the desert wind.

'no reason for what keeps happening
to them.' He sipped from a glass
of bokha* and explained how

from this same jetty, long before
the Arabs and Vandals, even before
the Romans and their famous theater,

boats filled with people and goods
and sailed off. A day or a week later,
the sea sends back the drowned.

His long-lashed eyes closed when
he spoke, his face unchanged by the years.
His fingers moved so carefully

putting out his cigarette. He saw me
looking, nodded, then pulled me toward
his manhood to help him sleep.

* a drink made of distilled fig juice.

Ramallah, Occupied West Bank

May 2018

Rayya Mohammed still had the huge, rusty key to the family home in Abu Shusha. It hung on a hook on the wall next to her late husband's walking stick – not that she expected ever to use it again. 'There's no way they will let us return,' she said. Aged eighty-two, she was wearing a traditional long black Palestinian dress decorated with red embroidery, and a white headscarf. Her sightless hazel eyes were filmy, and she gripped my hand as we sat on the sofa in her house in Ramallah. Since she had gone blind, she liked to touch anyone she talked to. I looked down at her bony hand, which held mine more tightly as she recounted the horror of what she had seen in 1948, when she was twelve. 'The Jews attacked our village three times, but when the battle got hard they fled,' she said. 'The fourth time they came to kill. They came with a big force, surrounded the village and killed the villagers, especially the youths. Some people escaped, while others were arrested.'

The massacres by Jewish brigades in the Arab-Israeli War that led to the founding of the state of Israel have been well documented. About 900 Palestinian Muslims lived in Abu Shusha. On 13th May 1948, the day before Israel declared independence, the Jewish Givati Brigade made its final attack on the village. They killed about seventy men. According to one Israeli historian, some were lined up and executed, others shot in the back and a few killed with axes.

Rayya hid in caves at the edge of the village, along with the other children and their mothers, before fleeing. 'We were afraid and hungry. The women were so sad – crying for their relatives, brothers and sons. I saw all this while we were fleeing,' she recalled. 'They were not killed in front of my eyes, but when we escaped, women began searching for their sons and husbands. My brothers were killed that same day. They killed, brutally, anyone who had a weapon. We couldn't recognise my brother's body. It took us four days to find him.'

Palestinians call the founding of the Jewish state the *nakba* – the catastrophe. All that remains of Abu Shusha is a pile of stones on a sparse hillside. Israelis sometimes go mountain-biking there. A new village, Pedaya, was founded nearby in 1951. Most of the residents are Jews who were expelled from Iraq. They say they know nothing of the massacre. 'War is war,' said Sabri Pinchas, whose family was driven out of Baghdad. 'I know that feeling because we were also like them – they fled their homes and escaped. We did, too.'

But the difference is stark. The Israelis feel that they are finally at home, in their own land, but Rayya could not feel that Ramallah was home as long as the Palestinian territories are occupied by Israel. In 2022 she died a refugee, with a key to a house that was destroyed long ago, in a village that no longer exists, in a country that remains a dream.

Many Sri Lankan Tamils, forced out of their homes during the long civil war, feel similarly. The largely Sinhalese army took control of their homes. For the Tamil poet Sharmila Seyyid, the keys to her childhood home have the same symbolic importance as they did for Rayya Mohammed.

Keys to an Empty Home

Sharmila Seyyid, 2015
Translated from the Tamil by
Lakshmi Holmström and Sascha Ebeling

There. That was my home,
the house where my mother gave birth to me
where my father carried me on his shoulders
and played with me.

They broke up this house;
we don't know why.
Yet the keys to the house we locked up
are still with us.

It was in the courtyard of that house
I wrote out the alphabet
for the very first time.

There, that was my home.
That neem tree you see by the side of the well –
it was there I played on my swing.
Look, a scrap of the red rope
from which the swing was hung
is still suspended there.

I have no idea why they did it,
what use my house was to them
I don't know;
but they broke it down.
Yet the keys to our locked-up house
still stay in our hands.

After the house was broken down
my father wept constantly
gazing at the keys
to the locked-up house.

Until he died, all he yearned for
was to lean against the walls of his house
peacefully, for one last time.
His love for his own house
was an empty dream.
Now my father is gone
and so is the house where
I clung to my father's shoulder.
Yet, the keys to the locked-up house
are still in our hands.

Goma, Democratic Republic of the Congo (then Zaire)

July 1994

The symptoms of cholera are easy to identify: white, watery stools and vomit, leading to such a rapid loss of fluids that the eyes begin to sink and the teeth protrude. It's easily cured by rehydration, administered either orally or intravenously, but where fresh water is scarce, cholera can kill in twelve hours. When a million refugees crossed the border from Rwanda to Goma, in what was then called Zaire, in a few days, the disease rampaged through the population with extraordinary speed. The sick collapsed in the main street, or on the fields of sharp black volcanic rock where makeshift camps had sprung up. They died where they fell. Bodies lay unburied, covered by a blanket. If you weren't careful, you might trip over one.

One morning I walked into a tent erected by an aid agency to see dozens of people sprawled semi-conscious around the edge, their eyes glassy, some drooling a thick saliva, family members sitting on the ground next to them, cradling their heads. A lone doctor stood in the middle, crying.

'They're just dying and dying,' she sobbed. 'What can I do?'

She had no drips left, nor any oral rehydration salts, nor – even more critically – a regular supply of clean water. I began to weep too, as we stood together watching people die.

The pitiful people dying had, a few days earlier, been killing. They were Hutus, Rwanda's majority ethnic group. That April, following the shooting down of a plane carrying the Rwandan president, also a Hutu, their leaders had instructed them to kill their neighbours from the minority Tutsi ethnic group. They had set to work immediately with machetes and clubs. Lawyers do not accept the idea of a collective crime, but a large proportion of the Hutu population, both men and women, played some part in the genocide. Now, a Tutsi-dominated guerrilla force, the Rwandan Patriotic Army, was about to take power, so the Hutu leadership had told their people to flee across the border.

The Hutus in Goma were generally referred to as refugees, but were they in fact fugitives? The cholera epidemic put them in a liminal and unrecognised category of both perpetrator and victim.

Every day journalists would visit the camps. One of my notes reads, 'Little girl sitting on the ground holding umbrella above her, cradling a baby in her arms. She starts to cry because the baby died.' After a few days, the refugees began to wrap their dead in rush matting shrouds and carry them to the side of the camps, where they neatly lined the edge of the road like pale kerbstones. The French military, which had been brought in to manage the chaos, dynamited the rock some way from the camps to make mass graves. I watched dump trucks tipping bodies into giant trenches filled with quicklime, sending up clouds of white powder which hung in the air before settling like snow on the death pits. No one talked about identifying the dead, let alone funerals or mourning rituals.

Cholera had spread rapidly because the refugees were drinking water from Lake Kivu, where the tiny, comma-shaped bacillus *Vibrio cholerae* lurked in the shallows. Eventually the aid agencies brought in clean water and medical supplies. The epidemic ran its course. Initially, it wasn't known how many had died because the truckers had been paid by the body and exaggerated the numbers they had transported to the mass graves. A World Health

Organization study later estimated that 50,000 people died in Goma in that period, 23,800 of them from cholera. Three decades on, when I close my eyes I can still see uncounted, lifeless, anonymous bodies. They are a nameless, largely forgotten multitude, just like the victims of the bubonic plague that ravaged London in 1665, evoked by the Victorian poet Christina Rossetti.

The Plague

Christina Rossetti, 1848

'Listen, the last stroke of death's noon has struck—
The plague is come,' a gnashing Madman said,
And laid him down straightway upon his bed.
His writhed hands did at the linen pluck;
Then all is over. With a careless chuck
Among his fellows he is cast. How sped
His spirit matters little: many dead
Make men hard-hearted.—'Place him on the truck.
Go forth into the burial-ground and find
Room at so much a pitful for so many.
One thing is to be done; one thing is clear:
Keep thou back from the hot unwholesome wind,
That it infect not thee.' Say, is there any
Who mourneth for the multitude dead here?

MEMORY

We guard the stain

'The struggle of man against power is the struggle of memory against forgetting,' wrote the Czech novelist Milan Kundera. Sometimes the powerful distort memory rather than erase it, rewriting history to make themselves the victims. Or they demand amnesia, in the hope that if enough years go by their crimes will dissolve into the ether of the past. But forgetfulness has its own virtue: the word 'amnesty' has the same Greek root as 'amnesia'. An individual may find it hard to forget, but political leaders can choose to give amnesty to former enemies, to help society's process of healing and reconciliation. Everyone who has been through war finds some experiences too painful to recall, but too searing to forget. The end of a war may leave people on all sides without purpose: that's why survivors must decide how to balance memory and forgetting as they try to learn to live in peace.

Louvain, Belgium

August 2014

Marie Legrand was three years old when German soldiers marched through Louvain, shot people dead on the streets and set the town ablaze. She was 103 when she told me the story. Elegant in a rose-pink silk suit and matching scarf, her mind had remained sharp, although it was impossible to know what she really remembered, and what had been imprinted by a lifetime of telling and retelling. 'I remember the sound of their boots marching past,' she said. 'They didn't know there was a whole society of children hidden underground.' Her father would hold his finger sternly to his lips and tell the children to be silent. 'He said if you don't obey, the Germans will kill you, so we obeyed.' Another memory floated into her mind. 'I remember the smell of smoke – it was everywhere,' she said. 'That was the smell of Louvain. The Germans had a terrible cruelty.'

Two thousand buildings were destroyed, 248 people killed and the entire population of 10,000 forced to flee. The great library, containing 300,000 medieval manuscripts, was burnt to the ground. In the nearby village of Dinant, German forces lined the citizens up and shot them, killing more than 600. But wandering round the placid town – now usually known by its Flemish name, Leuven – I found it hard to imagine the terror of August 1914. Ice cream cones in hand, tourists were sitting in pavement cafés and exploring the cobbled streets. A century is a long time.

The Germans justified their atrocities by blaming the Belgian resistance for an incident in which several German soldiers were killed. (In fact, it was probably friendly fire.) In her classic account of the first month of the First World War, *The Guns of August*, Barbara Tuchman writes: 'The Germans burned Louvain not as a punishment for alleged Belgian misdeeds, but as a deterrent and as a warning to all their enemies – a gesture of German might before the world.' German commanders allowed the soldiers to steal wine and beer from the town's cellars so many of them were roaring drunk as they lurched through the streets, looting and killing, hoping that terrified civilians would pressure their leaders to surrender.

Europe endured another war before Germany's ambitions were curtailed and the countries settled into first an uneasy and then a real peace. Prosperity saved Belgium, backed up by the institutions, including the European Union, that were established after the Second World War. I asked Marie if she still feared the Germans or nurtured any feelings of hatred. 'It's a waste of time. Close the page. Forget it,' she replied. 'If you carry hatred and vengeance with you, then you'll never have peace.'

The peace western Europe has enjoyed since the First and Second World Wars seems remarkable compared to the smouldering resentments, sporadic violence and frozen conflicts that have continued elsewhere. Dunya Mikhail, an Iraqi-American poet, dreams that one day her country might be like Belgium where peace is so ordinary it's taken for granted.

The Iraqi Nights (*extract*)

Dunya Mikhail, 2013
Translated from the Arabic by
Kareem James Abu-Zeid

In Iraq,
after a thousand and one nights,
someone will talk to someone else.
Markets will open
for regular customers.
Small feet will tickle
the giant feet of the Tigris.
Gulls will spread their wings
and no one will fire at them.
Women will walk the streets
without looking back in fear.
Men will give their real names
without putting their lives at risk.
Children will go to school
and come home again.
Chickens in the villages
won't peck at human flesh
on the grass.
Disputes will take place
without any explosives.
A cloud will pass over cars

heading to work as usual.
A hand will wave
to someone leaving
or returning.
The sunrise will be the same
for those who wake
and those who never will.
And every moment
something ordinary
will happen
under the sun.

South Sudan

December 1988

How many of the people I have interviewed in warzones over the years have I forgotten? Dozens? Hundreds? Old notebooks and articles may jog my memory, but my own amnesia reflects a broader reality: most victims of war go unremembered except by their closest relatives, who may soon also become victims. It's estimated that two million people have died in South Sudan, mostly of disease and hunger, during a series of civil wars from the 1950s until today. They remain nameless to the wider world, and go largely unmourned.

When the war between the government in Khartoum and the forces of the Sudan People's Liberation Army (SPLA) was at its height in the 1980s, I used to visit every few months from the Kenyan capital, Nairobi, where I lived. While the regional capital, Juba, was in government hands, the SPLA controlled the rural area beyond the city limits. To avoid being shot down over rebel-held territory, the pilot would continue at altitude to Juba's airspace and then corkscrew down to the tiny airport. Any fear I might have felt was quickly overwhelmed by motion sickness. The SPLA was fighting for independence, and in 2011, after negotiations and a referendum, South Sudan became the world's youngest country. But the fighting never stopped – it's now between different tribes and factions within the new country's government. South Sudanese are still being forced to flee their homes and dying of the poverty that war and corruption reinforce.

In December 1988 I met a teacher called Lapir Luke Nyeko. I don't recall his face, but a story I wrote at the time says he and his wife and three children lived in a small mud house on the edge of a camp for displaced people in Juba. One day, on his way back from collecting firewood in the forest, he was captured by armed men of the SPLA. They said he must be a government supporter because he lived in the capital, so they beat him before stealing his bicycle and watch. Then they let him go. A few days later, his wife and children tried to return to their village, thinking it might be safer, but they were stopped on the way by government soldiers who stole everything they had: a bedsheet, some clothes and a piece of soap. 'Both sides hate us,' said Lapir, and it was hard to disagree with him.

I tell this story not because it was exceptional, but because it was so ordinary. That's why I don't remember Lapir Luke Nyeko – I heard versions of his experience multiple times. Being a journalist, I tell myself that the act of documenting someone's story makes it count for something, or at least for something more than if it had never been recorded at all. In my darker moments, I wonder. As the Iraqi poet Sargon Boulos puts it, the wind erases the traces of most killed in conflict.

News About No One

Sargon Boulus, 2001
Translated from the Arabic by the poet

Those who are
          never in the news,
whom no one remembers –
what wind erased their traces
as if they never walked the earth;
my father, all the others, where
          O where . . . ?

What happened to the
          neighbourhood carpenter
maker of solid beds, and dressers
          for brides?
How he worshipped the wood!

Where is the silent shoemaker
who hugged his anvil, and bit the bitter nails
between his teeth? Did a 'smart' bomb
demolish his hole-in-the-wall
crammed to the ceiling
with battered shoes?

Where the coppersmith,
        where the golden tray?

The ear of wheat around the saint's image?
The horseshoe above the door?
What happened to Umm Youssef, the midwife?
How many babies were dragged
    out of the warm darkness of the womb
into the starkness of this world
    by her dextrous hands
sending them on their way
    with a slap on their bare bottoms
through the crooked valleys of
        their destinies, soldiers who fight
        in dubious battles
        and unjust wars? . . .

After they got tired
slaving in the mills of poverty
to fill the granaries of the tyrant
did they feel ashamed of the way
        this world is made?

After the sieges, after the wars
beyond hunger, beyond
        enemies, out of the reach
of the executioner's hand –
        did they go to sleep
at last?
To sleep, and hug the dust.

Balagwe, Zimbabwe

September 2019

Unquiet spirits stalk the land of Zimbabwe. They cannot be calm until the right ceremonies have been performed, their bones taken to a place where they can be laid to rest. Until then, they plague their relatives, causing ill health and other problems. 'It is very painful,' said Ketty Maposa. 'Right now I am feeling sick, but I have no one to tell my troubles to. If I knew where my father's grave was I could kneel beside it and tell him my problems. But I don't know where it is.'

We were sitting in the yard of the small brick house in rural Matabeleland where she lived with her elderly mother and six children. Chickens pecked the dirt, and a harsh sun had baked the earth pale brown. It was nearly thirty years since soldiers dragged Ketty's father from their house and put him in their car. The family never saw him again. He was a victim of the *Gukurahundi* – 'the rain that washes away the chaff' – a campaign of massacres against the Ndebele people carried out by the government of Robert Mugabe in the early 1980s. The Fifth Brigade, trained by the North Koreans, swept across Matabeleland and murdered some 20,000 people. The aim was to wipe out enough of those who supported Mugabe's rivals to ensure that he could govern without effective opposition. It worked. He ruled for thirty-seven years.

Many of the victims of the *Gukurahundi* were killed at the Fifth Brigade's camp at Balagwe. Initially their bodies were stuffed down a mineshaft; later, their bones were cast into a mass grave.

Even in 2019, two years after Mugabe had been ousted at the age of ninety-three, state security agents destroyed a memorial plaque erected by the relatives of the dead at Balagwe. The families needed remembrance, and proper burial, but the state demanded amnesia.

Western journalists understand little of the spirit world, and rarely report its power – a huge void in understanding. A *n'anga*, a witch doctor, told me that Mugabe had consulted him to find out how he might quieten the spirits of Herbert Chitepo and Josiah Tongogara, two comrades whose murders he had ordered because he feared they might rival him as leader. Every Zimbabwean knows that Mugabe used to talk to the spirits. A survivor of the *Gukurahundi* smiled when I asked him shortly after Mugabe's death whether he would rest in peace. 'Not so much,' he said.

Zimbabwe's spirits may seem strange to non-Africans, but they are a manifestation of the universal need to commemorate publicly and privately those who die violent deaths. In villages across Britain, soldiers who lost their lives in the world wars are listed on memorials. States tend to be less keen on monuments for the civilian victims of massacres that they carried out. Construction of the Memorial to the Murdered Jews of Europe in Berlin didn't start until 2003. Andrea Cohen's poem about victims of the atomic bomb dropped by the US on Hiroshima speaks to the need to commemorate – to guard the stain that violence imprints on a people.

Explanation (Hiroshima)

Andrea Cohen, 2015

You have to explain
to the new girl, you

always do, to the one
who means, staying late,

to scrub the stain
from the marble stair

displayed at the museum.
You have to explain

that the darkness is not
a stain she can erase.

Rather, it's shade
and shadow, a stranglehold

that's all that's left
of a girl and boy who

sat on the school stair
as children do, and vanished.

You have to explain:
we guard the stain.

Krak des Chevaliers, Syria

March 2014

As I peered out through a slit in the three-metre-thick fortress wall, I thought about the archers and snipers who had done the same over the centuries. From the hill on which Krak des Chevaliers stands you can survey miles of desert, farmland and villages. The modern Syrian city of Homs lies twenty-five miles to the east, and the Lebanese border to the south. It's a huge stone structure, seemingly impregnable. Fighters of the Islamic State had been its most recent occupants – the debris of their presence was everywhere: water bottles, a jerrycan, a red and white prayer mat. The Emir of Aleppo built the castle in the eleventh century, and then the religious-military Crusader order, the Knights Hospitaller, fortified it further. From the castle, the Crusaders repelled the forces of the great Muslim leader Saladin, then in 1271 they were defeated and the Mamluks took control.

Bombs and artillery wreak more damage than crossbows and battle-axes. T. E. Lawrence – later known as Lawrence of Arabia – who visited in 1909, described Krak des Chevaliers as 'the most complete and admirable castle in the world', but we had to scramble over rubble where parts of the inner wall had been destroyed. Unconcerned by the damage they were doing, Syrian government forces had bombed the castle repeatedly from the air in their attempt to oust the IS fighters. The moment of history in which they were living was more important to them than preserving emblems of the country's past. We found signs that the Islamists had used the Crusader church as a living room with their families – scattered children's shoes and clothing. I picked up a small silver spoon, decorated with a blue glass bead, which they must have used to stir the sugar in their tea. They had left in a hurry, as others had done over the centuries.

The latest victors, soldiers of the Syrian army, were taking up residence, carrying mattresses and blankets into the fortress just as the Crusaders, the Mamluks and the jihadis had done – generations of young men fighting for religion and country. Protected by the vast walls, all must have felt invincible in their time, but no regime lasts forever. The fortress, like the desert it surveys and the rocks on which it stands, is timeless. Whatever the damage wrought by this latest conflict, Krak des Chevaliers will outlast them all. The Kurdish-Turkish poet Bejan Matur expresses that thought in four simple Turkish words – five in translation.

Truth (2017)

Bejan Matur
Translated from the Turkish by
Canan Marasligil with Jen Hadfield

What stones know
                      humankind
forgets

Arusha, Tanzania

January 1997

The accused, dressed in a dark jacket, sat impassively staring ahead, just a few yards from me in the airless, sweltering court-room. The allegations: genocide and crimes against humanity. Jean-Paul Akayesu had been mayor of Taba, in central Rwanda, while villagers and militia under his control slaughtered thou-sands of people with farm implements and crude home-made weapons. His was the first case to be heard by the International Criminal Tribunal for Rwanda (ICTR) in Arusha, Tanzania. Three years had passed since the Rwandan genocide, and now I was taking the stand as a witness for the prosecution.

Emmanuel Rudasingwa had been planning to testify, too, but he was murdered before he could do so. His widow, Godelième Mukasarasi, thought she knew why. Rudasingwa ran a small local shop and was brave enough to talk to the tribunal investigators who visited the area. 'Everyone knew Emmanuel was talking because they saw a big car outside the door,' she said. Akayesu's defenders were determined that anyone who knew anything about the campaign to wipe out the Tutsi people in Taba would not make it to court in Arusha.

To protect sources and their own reputation as unbiased wit-nesses, journalists have gone to gaol for not testifying in court about information they have gained in the course of their report-ing. But as the only foreign correspondent living in Kigali in the first few days of the genocide, I had been in a unique position. I was an eyewitness from the very beginning of the slaughter. I didn't know if Akayesu himself was guilty, but the prosecution wanted me to testify that any alleged crimes were part of a 'widespread and systematic' campaign to kill civilians for reasons of ethnicity, race, religion or politics. Of that I had no doubt.

The ICTR was inadequate. It failed to protect witnesses like Emmanuel Rudasingwa, and it didn't prosecute members of the Rwandan Patriotic Front (RPF) which had put an end to the genocide against the Tutsis by taking over the country but had in turn murdered many thousands of people. Still, before winding up at the end of 2015, the tribunal convicted sixty-one people, including not only bureaucrats like Akayesu, but also the most significant political and military leaders responsible for the genocide.

I told the court what I saw after the plane carrying President Juvénal Habyarimana was shot down over Kigali on 6th April 1994, when soldiers and extremist militia from the Hutu majority started to massacre members of the Tutsi minority and Hutus who opposed the government. I described the hundreds of hacked bodies spilling out of the morgue, the blood running down the hospital drains, the baby whose leg had been partially severed by a machete, the drunken soldiers and young men on roadblocks. I recounted how Tutsis I knew rang me sobbing in terror, saying prowling gangs of armed Hutu militia were threatening to kill them.

Unlike Rwandan villagers, I was not risking my life by testifying. If they had the courage to speak, I didn't see how I could refuse. But I also did it because I happened to witness one of the most brutal mass crimes of the twentieth century. Justice provided some kind of reckoning, even as the world moved on, and Rwandans tried to rebuild their country and their shattered lives. By putting what I had seen on the record in a court of law, I was trying to put history to rest.

Wisława Szymborska's poem mentions journalists like me who

move from one conflict to the next. But war leaves its stain on us too. We too watch as memory fades, and the stories are told by 'those who know little. / And less than little. / And finally as little as nothing.' We hope that, whether in books, news programmes, articles or a court of law, the testimony of those of us who saw with our own eyes what happened will count for something in the battle between memory and forgetting.

The End and the Beginning

Wisława Szymborska, 1993
Translated from the Polish by
Joanna Trzeciak

After every war
someone has to clean up.
Things won't
straighten themselves up, after all.

Someone has to push the rubble
to the side of the road,
so the corpse-filled wagons
can pass.

Someone has to get mired
in scum and ashes,
sofa springs,
splintered glass,
and bloody rags.

Someone has to drag in a girder
to prop up a wall.
Someone has to glaze a window,
rehang a door.

Photogenic it's not,
and takes years.
All the cameras have left
for another war.

We'll need the bridges back,
and new railway stations.
Sleeves will go ragged
from rolling them up.

Someone, broom in hand,
still recalls the way it was.
Someone else listens
and nods with unsevered head.
But already there are those nearby
starting to mill about
who will find it dull.

From out of the bushes
sometimes someone still unearths
rusted-out arguments
and carries them to the garbage pile.

Those who knew
what was going on here
must make way for
those who know little.
And less than little.
And finally as little as nothing.

In the grass that has overgrown
causes and effects,
someone must be stretched out
blade of grass in his mouth
gazing at the clouds.

Afterword

While writing and compiling this volume a question has hung over me: is this an anti-war book? In one sense, of course it is. It's about suffering and death and futility, all the terrible things that characterise conflict. But it's not a book that marches down the street with a placard shouting, 'Stop the War!' I believe people and countries have the right – even the responsibility – to defend themselves, and that sometimes the only way to dislodge a dictator is by armed insurrection. Still, experience tells me that war never turns out as planned, and taints everyone it touches. Revolutionary leaders who initially seemed romantic and righteous become venal and cruel; leaders resisting invasion use misleading propaganda; what starts as self-defence ends up as slaughter. The online world increasingly demands binary attitudes: you're with us or against us, and sympathy for victims on the other side is tantamount to treachery. Inconsistency may be the only authentic response – the writer Robert Graves said Siegfried Sassoon 'varied between happy warrior and bitter pacifist'.

'Unhappy is the land that needs a hero,' wrote Bertolt Brecht. But heroes do not all have to be soldiers – poets may also fit the bill. A statue of Taras Shevchenko, with his massive, drooping moustache, stands in nearly every town I have visited in Ukraine. The reputation of the national poet, who wrote revolutionary verse in the nineteenth century, has been further elevated by the 2022 Russian invasion. In Borodyanka, a small town near the Ukrainian capital Kyiv that saw some of the worst of the early fighting, he surveys a bombed out apartment block, the windows blackened and broken. More than 150 years on, his struggle is not yet won.

In his poem 'In Memory of W. B. Yeats', W. H. Auden wrote:

For poetry makes nothing happen: it survives
In the valley of its making where executives
Would never want to tamper, flows on south
From ranches of isolation and the busy griefs,
Raw towns that we believe and die in; it survives,
A way of happening, a mouth.

In other words, poetry doesn't have to express a political message, the form itself speaks to people, crystallising their reality without necessarily changing it. Poets are amongst the most respected intellectuals in the Arab world, where references to traditional verse, including from the Koran, are often incorporated into everyday speech. Almost every Somali is a poet, I'm told – the fact that the language wasn't written down until 1973 means the practice of recitation remains strong, and decades of conflict have fuelled creative fires. War brings people closer to their poets. Focussing on physical suffering, journalists often fail to see the importance of art to people struggling to preserve their humanity. Mental health and trauma have become a focus, but we often fail to recognise people's spiritual and religious needs, to perceive the yearning for the comfort of ritual and recitation.

Refugees bring only what they can carry, which frequently means songs, stories, poems and prayers that they know by heart. They can't go back, not just because it's dangerous, but because the country they grew up in no longer exists – war changes everything. They are lost in both space and time. Verses learnt at your grandmother's knee or in school are anchors to the old life and provide a source of strength and identity that gives solace in an alien and often hostile world. Some of the best war poetry is written in exile.

> *Fear and the muse take turns to guard*
> *the room where the exiled poet is banished*

So wrote Anna Akhmatova for her friend and fellow poet Osip Mandelstam who was sent into internal exile by Stalin in 1934 and died in a labour camp four years later. Their poems about war and oppression are amongst the most powerful of the twentieth century.

Poetry doesn't have to reflect what's current, and may take inspiration from conflicts that took place centuries past. Eyewitness journalists, by contrast, have to be there. War corresponding has by its nature always been a dangerous occupation, and it is getting more so. The Committee to Protect Journalists says sixty-nine journalists were killed in the Second World War and sixty-three in Vietnam, but no conflict has killed so many journalists so quickly as the war in Gaza. According to the CPJ, by June 2024 a horrifying 108 had been killed, 103 of them Palestinians, some seemingly targeted by Israel. (In Gaza, poets were not spared either: at the time of writing, at least thirteen have been killed. Mosab Abu Toha was briefly detained by Israeli forces in Gaza. After escaping to Cairo in December 2023, his poetry gained an added urgency and anger.)

Every warlord or dictator watches what journalists broadcast and reads what we write. We can no longer persuade them to give us an interview by saying we will tell the world what they say, because they can communicate directly through their own propaganda channels. Moreover, they know that we want to expose the human rights abuses they're committing, and don't care if we're 'objective' and are exposing the other side's atrocities too. We may see ourselves as a tribe apart, not representatives of our governments, but that distinction gets lost. The Islamic State regards western reporters as bargaining chips to be kidnapped for ransom or envoys from the enemy to be murdered. Russian reporters, funded by an exiled businessman, who tried to uncover the activities of the mercenary Wagner Group in the Central African Republic in 2018 wound up dead. Killing the messenger is not a metaphor.

It's not just increased danger that makes it harder. Western culture has grown resistant to our stories. 'Go, go, go,' said T. S. Eliot's bird in 'Burnt Norton'. 'Humankind cannot bear very much reality.' A strange inversion of modern times is that while on the TV news we are allowed to show less and less of the real horror – the broken bodies, the blood, the vultures gathering over abandoned corpses – computer games are ever more violent, with players experiencing killing as a risk-free fantasy. Before my Channel 4 News stories, the presenter often says, 'Viewers may find some of the images in this report distressing.' It's a cue to look away, but I want viewers to keep watching. They *should* be distressed; war is distressing. I don't want to show a sanitised version, nor boost the idea that violence is just a game.

Gaming technology has fed into real warfare, with people behind computers thousands of miles from the battle zone locating targets for airstrikes. In Afghanistan, groups of Taliban or other insurgents identified by US drone operators on fuzzy screens sometimes turned out to be wedding parties or other civilian gatherings. In a notorious incident, as US forces were pulling out after the Taliban takeover in 2021, a Hellfire missile, released from a Reaper drone (the clues are in the names), killed a family including seven children near Kabul Airport. The Americans were trying to target a man who had killed civilians with a bomb in the area a few days earlier. Reporters in Kabul rushed to the scene to take pictures, ask people what had happened and establish the identities of those who had been killed. The Pentagon obfuscated for days, but could not deny what journalists had seen with their own eyes and heard recounted by those who had been there. This is why journalists have to be on the ground, to confront the remote targeters and their commanding officers with the consequences of their mistakes.

Eyewitness reports from journalists have renewed significance now many people get their news from social media, where the algorithm directs them towards a version of events that reinforces their point of view. Those scrolling through online feeds often fail to distinguish between a reporter in the field bringing challenging or unwelcome news and an armchair warrior or political propagandist who tells them what they want to hear. 'News literacy' – understanding how the media works, and how to decipher sources of information – has become as important as maths but is still not taught in schools.

Nonetheless, new technology has its upsides: working from a distance, journalists can analyse opensource satellite imagery to see concentrations of troops preparing to invade, which we did as Russian troops massed on the Ukrainian borders in early 2022. They can geolocate viral videos of atrocities and compare the images that governments publicise with other online sources. I am an on-the-ground journalist – being there, asking questions, testing everything I observe against an understanding of geopolitics and diplomacy born of experience. But when reporters like me are denied visas, or barred from a front line because the military doesn't want us to see what's happening (military press officers always say 'it's for your own safety'), or can only see one part of the bigger picture, a new breed of online investigative journalists who have never been near a warzone are uncovering what's going on.

Marie Colvin believed in the power of journalism to 'make a difference'. Being unable to point to an occasion when my own reporting has altered the course of history, I am less ambitious. I want to draw attention to neglected conflicts as well as those that capture daily headlines, which is why I went to Sudan in mid 2024. Although Gaza was more intense, and Ukraine had greater geo-strategic importance, it was in Sudan where the largest number of people were in danger – 10 million forced to flee their homes and 19 million threatened with famine, because of a futile conflict that had its roots in a struggle for power between two stubborn warlords, that was now being fuelled by regional powers. I believe it's important for journalists, using whatever tools we have, to uncover what is being covered up, to counter the lies that are always told in times of war and – as far as we can – show the truth of what is happening, however unpopular that makes us. It matters not least because more war is coming: the conflicts and refugee flows caused by climate change are only just starting, while western societies are riven by polarising political discourse that threatens to spill over into more violence. Artificial intelligence has a terrifying potential to disassociate further those who make the decision to kill from those who are killed, and enable propagandists to fake images. It's our job to sound warnings and cut through dangerous rhetoric. Even if our reporting changes nothing, when it's over politicians should not be able to say that they didn't know. They knew because we told them.

On the whole, though, journalism is ephemeral. We rarely read the stories written by reporters who covered the First and Second World Wars. We do, of course, read the poetry. So, I suspect, will it be today. Journalists focus on what is critical now – this village taken, that truce broken, a new atrocity by occupying forces. But poets through the ages have turned the horror of war into transcendent works of beauty and meaning.

Journalism is of the moment. But poetry lasts forever.

Chronology of Conflicts

There is no room for a detailed account of each conflict I have covered, but these brief notes might serve as a rough reference guide. Many other wars have occurred in my lifetime, and some of these countries have experienced several, but I have concentrated on those I witnessed and have written about in this book. Many, unfortunately, have a start date but no end – the details are as accurate as possible at the time of writing.

Belgium, 1914–18
Germany invaded Belgium in August 1914 and occupied it until the end of the First World War. Much of the trench warfare occurred along the Western Front, which included Belgium, Luxembourg and France. During the conflict, Germany, Austria-Hungary, Bulgaria and the Ottoman Empire (the Central Powers) fought against Great Britain, France, Russia, Italy, Romania, Canada, Japan and the United States (the Allied Powers). Some historians see the end as just a pause before the Second World War when Germany again invaded other European countries.

Israel/Palestine, 1948–
The year 1948 saw the creation of the State of Israel on land which had been administered under British mandate and known as Palestine. Palestinians call it the *nakba*, the catastrophe. Both Arab Palestinians and Jews lay claim to the territory, citing historical and religious rights. After the Six-Day War in 1967, Israel occupied parts

of what had then been Jordan – now the Occupied West Bank – and the Gaza Strip which had previously been administered by Egypt. A lengthy peace process in the 1980s and 90s failed. In October 2023, Hamas fighters broke out of Gaza, killed more than a thousand Israeli citizens and kidnapped others. Israel announced a state of war, bombing and invading Gaza, causing tens of thousands of Palestinian deaths and destroying homes, universities, schools, hospitals and places of religious and historical significance. The possibility of a 'two-state solution', where Israel and an independent Palestine live side by side in peace, appears distant.

Sudan, 1956–

Sudan has been through several civil wars since gaining independence from Britain in 1956. Brigadier-General Omar al-Bashir seized power in a coup in 1989; under his rule, war with the southern part of the country continued until 2005. Other separatist groups also fought the government, including in Darfur in 2003 where African groups mounted a rebellion. In response, Al-Bashir armed an Arab militia, known as the *Janjaweed*, which committed many atrocities. Some 200,000 people, mostly civilians, were killed. Al-Bashir was ousted in a civilian uprising in 2019. A coup in 2021 brought the army back to power. Two years later, war broke out between the Sudanese Armed Forces and the Rapid Support Forces, the successor to the *Janjaweed*.

South Sudan, 1956–

Armed rebel groups started to fight the government in Khartoum even before independence in 1956. Since 1983, when the Sudan People's Liberation Army (SPLA) was formed, some two million people are estimated to have been killed by war, famine and disease while at least four million were displaced. After the end of hostilities in 2005, and independence in 2011, South Sudan became the youngest and one of the poorest countries in the world. The government was led by the political wing of the SPLA. When the country's leaders fell out in 2013, a new civil war started.

Uganda, 1980–86
Uganda was plagued by violence, civil war and outside intervention after independence from Britain in 1962. Some 200,000 people were killed after President Milton Obote took power from Idi Amin in 1980, in a series of massacres carried out by the national army in the Luwero Triangle, north of the main city, Kampala. The National Resistance Army (NRA), led by Yoweri Museveni, started a guerrilla war in 1980, which lasted until 1986 when they defeated Obote's successor, Tito Okello.

Zimbabwe, 1981–2
After independence in 1980, when Rhodesia became Zimbabwe, Prime Minister (later President) Robert Mugabe decided to curb the influence of his former comrade-in-arms Joshua Nkomo. The two men had both headed rebel armies that fought white minority rule, but were now political rivals. Mugabe was from the majority Shona tribe, while Nkomo was an Ndebele from Matabeleland. Mugabe sent troops to Matabeleland to kill Nkomo's supporters. The massacres are known as *Gukurahundi* – the wind that blows away the chaff. Nkomo died in 1999. Mugabe remained in power until 2017, and died two years later.

Mexico, 1990–
Mexican drug cartels increased their power and wealth after the demise of the Colombian cartels in the 1990s. While a majority of drugs entering the USA come from Mexico, most of the weapons used by those involved in the drug trade originate in the US where gun laws are lax. More than 300,000 Mexicans are estimated to have been killed in the drug wars – some in confrontations with the authorities, and others in wars between different cartels.

Bosnia, 1992–95

The Bosnian Civil War was triggered by the breakup of Yugoslavia at the end of the Cold War. It was a three-cornered struggle between Serbs, Croats and Bosnian Muslims, now often called Bosniaks. Pogroms against Bosniaks by the Yugoslav National Army and local ethnic Serbs gave rise to the term 'ethnic cleansing'. The most notorious mass crime of the war, the killing by Serb forces of 7,000 Bosniak boys and men at Srebrenica, was deemed a 'crime of genocide' by the International Criminal Tribunal for the Former Yugoslavia. The war ended with the Dayton Accords, a peace agreement brokered by the US, the European Union and Russia.

Rwanda, 1994

The genocide in Rwanda started after a plane carrying the president was brought down over Kigali Airport. Immediately, the leaders of a faction known as Hutu Power ordered people from the majority Hutu community to murder their Tutsi neighbours. The genocide was stopped by the Rwandan Patriotic Front (RPF), a mainly Tutsi force that had been fighting the Hutu government since 1990. By the time the RPF took power, some 800,000 people, mainly Tutsis, had been killed. More than a million Hutus fled the country. In the aftermath, the RPF committed revenge killings. The subsequent wars in the neighbouring Democratic Republic of the Congo were caused in part by violence spreading from Rwanda.

Kosovo, 1998–99

Kosovo remained part of Serbia after the breakup of Yugoslavia, despite having an ethnic Albanian majority. After the war in Bosnia, the Kosovo Liberation Army (KLA) stepped up its war for independence, while Serbian forces committed a series of atrocities against Kosovar Albanians. NATO forces intervened to protect the Albanians. After an eleven-week NATO bombing campaign, Serbian forces withdrew from Kosovo which then came under temporary UN administration. Kosovo declared independence in 2008.

Ethiopia/Eritrea, 1998–2000
Two guerrilla groups, the Tigray People's Liberation Front (TPLF) and the Eritrean People's Liberation Front (EPLF) fought together in the 1970s and 80s to defeat the Ethiopian dictator Mengistu Haile Mariam. After Mengistu was ousted in 1991, the TPLF leader, Meles Zenawi, became Ethiopian president, while Eritrea gained independence under the EPLF leader, Isaias Afewerki. At first, Ethiopia and the new state of Eritrea lived peacefully as neighbours, but in 1998, each claimed a small piece of territory around the border town of Badme. At least 70,000 people are believed to have been killed in the subsequent conflict. A peace treaty signed in 2000 wasn't fully implemented until 2018. In 2020, war broke out again within Ethiopia, and conflicts between different ethnic groups continue.

Chechnya, 1999–2009
The First Chechen War, which started in 1994, ended in a peace treaty with Russia two years later. However, Chechen warlords carried out terror attacks in Russia in a continuation of their struggle for independence. The Second Chechen War started in 1999 after Vladimir Putin became Russian prime minister. An indiscriminate bombing campaign by Russia caused the total destruction of the Chechen capital, Grozny, and dealt a fatal blow to Chechen separatist groups. Eventually Russia installed a pro-Moscow leader, Ramzan Kadyrov, as Chechen leader.

Afghanistan, 2001–2021

The Taliban, which adheres to a fundamentalist Islamist code including the subjugation of women, took power in 1996. They gave sanctuary to al-Qaeda, a largely Arab jihadi group, and its leader Osama bin Laden, which used Afghanistan as a base to plan the September 2001 attacks in New York and Washington known as 9/11. The US, with allies including the UK, subsequently invaded Afghanistan and overthrew the Taliban. For twenty years, the US and its allies provided money and military support to successive Afghan governments, but the Taliban continued to resist as a guerrilla force. The departure of US troops in 2021 led to the collapse of the Afghan government they had supported and the return to power of the Taliban.

Global War on Terror, 2001–2021

The Global War on Terror (GWOT) was announced by US President George W. Bush after 9/11 when jihadis from al-Qaeda attacked the US by crashing planes into the World Trade Center in New York. The phrase was used to cover the subsequent invasions of Afghanistan and Iraq, and continuing attempts to prevent terror attacks especially in Europe. It can be regarded as having finished when US troops pulled out of Afghanistan, although governments remain on alert for jihadist terrorism.

Iraq, 2003–2019

In 1991, after the Iraqi dictator, Saddam Hussein, invaded neighbouring Kuwait, a US-led coalition drove him out. However, it did not topple him. In 2003, a similar coalition invaded Iraq again, purportedly because Saddam had weapons of mass destruction but also because the US regarded his continued rule as a destabilising factor in the region. However, despite the presence of US occupying troops until 2011, neighbouring Iran gained more influence, and Iraq entered a period of greater instability. The Islamic State originated in Iraq, seizing a large swathe of the country in 2014, which it united with part of Syria and called the Caliphate. Some 300,000 people are estimated to have been killed in Iraq since the 2003 US invasion.

Libya, 2011–

In 2011, uprisings against dictatorship known as the Arab Spring swept across the Middle East, reaching eastern Libya in February. Colonel Muammar Gaddafi, who had seized power in a coup in 1969, had dismantled an already weak state and ruled by violent whim. Although his forces were rapidly driven from the east of the country, they held on in the west and war continued until he was killed in August. Libya then descended into anarchy, as there were no institutions to replace the strongman, and a medley of competing militia controlled different parts of the country. Instability spread west across the Sahel, leading to more Africans trying to leave for Europe via Libya's Mediterranean ports.

Syria, 2011–

President Bashar al-Assad used extreme violence to crush Arab Spring protests in Syria. Rebel groups, some funded and armed by Gulf states, then seized territory and revolution morphed into civil war. Some groups were nationalist rather than religious, but the Islamic State moved in, governing part of northern Syria and Iraq which they called the Caliphate. By 2023, between 350,000 and 600,000 people are believed to have been killed, and 12 million displaced. Idlib, which borders Turkey, remained in rebel hands and the Kurdish area in the north-east, known as Rojava, retained some autonomy, while Bashar al-Assad continued to hold power in Damascus.

Mali, 2012–

In 2012, Tuaregs – some of whom had come from Libya after the fall of Gaddafi – declared an independent state in northern Mali. They cooperated with jihadis, including some from the al-Qaeda branch in neighbouring Algeria. In 2013, troops from the former colonial power, France, intervened to help the Malian army defeat both groups. Then the UN launched a stabilisation mission known as MINUSMA. Although both the Tuaregs and jihadis were initially suppressed, further jihadi violence followed. The government was ousted in a military coup. After popular protests against the French, in 2021 a second military government invited in a Russian private military company, the Wagner Group. The last French forces left in 2022, followed by MINUSMA. The number of jihadi attacks has continued to increase.

Niger, 2015–

A swathe of countries in the Sahel – Mali, Burkina Faso and Niger – have been destabilised by a combination of arms inflows, land disputes exacerbated by climate change, and jihadi groups including al-Qaeda and the Islamic State. In 2015, jihadis who controlled parts of Mali came across the border and started to recruit young men who could no longer herd livestock because of desertification. Jihadis from Nigeria also moved back and forth across the border. In 2023, a coup ousted the elected government. The new military regime expelled forces from France, the former colonial power, which had been invited in by the civilian government to help combat the jihadis.

Ukraine, 2014–

When the Soviet Union collapsed in 1991, Ukraine declared independence. The main division in Ukrainian politics was between those who wanted to join the European Union, and those who favoured continuing close ties with Russia. In 2014, a popular uprising ousted a fraudulently elected pro-Russian leader. Russian forces then invaded, annexing Crimea and supporting puppet separatist movements in the Donbas region on the Russia border. By 2015, the conflict was largely frozen. In February 2022, Russian forces made a full-scale invasion of Ukraine, trying unsuccessfully to capture the capital, Kyiv. Russia then annexed parts of eastern Ukraine that it had occupied, leading to a prolonged conflict. Ukraine is backed and armed by the US and European countries.

Brief Notes on Poets

Abou Kerech, Amineh, 2004–
The winner of the 2017 John Betjeman Poetry Prize for poets aged 10–13, Abou Kerech and her family fled Syria when she was eight, settling in Oxford four years later. Her poetry was featured in *England; Poems From a School*, an anthology edited by her teacher, Kate Clanchy.

Abu Toha, Mosab, 1992–
Born and brought up in Gaza, Abu Toha's first collection, *Things You May Find Hidden in My Ear: Poems from Gaza*, won the 2022 Palestine Book Award, an American Book Award and the Derek Walcott Prize for Poetry. Abu Toha was also a finalist for a National Book Critics Circle Award. He is the founder of the Edward Said Library in Gaza and a contributor to the *New Yorker* and his essays won an OPC Flora Lewis Award in 2024. In November 2023, Abu Toha was detained/kidnapped by Israeli troops before leaving Gaza with his wife and children.

Al-Maghout, Mohammed, 1934–2006
Often called the father of Arabic free verse, the Syrian poet al-Maghout's first poems were written on cigarette papers while in prison in the 1950s. An independent voice for liberty and justice in the Arab world, he also wrote for theatre, TV and cinema.

Akhmatova, Anna, 1889–1966
Sometimes described as Russia's greatest modern poet, Akhmatova's poems reflect the turbulent times in which she lived, from the Great War and the Bolshevik Revolution to the Second World War. Refusing to leave Russia during Stalin's purges of dissidents and intellectuals, she had to memorise rather than write down her poetry.

Amelina, Victoria, 1986–2023
The author of two novels and a children's book, Amelina turned to poetry and began to investigate war crimes after the Russian invasion of Ukraine in 2022. She was killed in a Russian missile attack on a restaurant in the eastern Ukrainian town of Kramatorsk.

Amichai, Yehuda, 1924–2000
Born in Germany, Amichai moved with his family to Palestine in 1935. He fought in the British Army during the Second World War and later in the Israeli army. His poems have been translated from Hebrew into more than forty languages.

Auden, W. H., 1907–73
Often considered Britain's greatest twentieth-century poet, Auden is famed for the variety of poetic styles he used and the breadth of his subject matter. His poetry is often concerned with moral issues, as well as emotional and political themes. He won the Pulitzer Prize in 1948 and influenced generations of poets.

Benson, Fiona, 1978–
The winner of Britain's Forward Prize for her 2019 collection *Vertigo & Ghost*, which took as its theme the rape narrative in Ovid's *Metamorphoses*, Benson often features female experience, including motherhood, loss and war.

Boland, Eavan, 1944–2020
As one of the foremost female voices in Irish literature, Boland examines women's public and private experience of violence in her poetry. She won numerous prizes and taught at both Trinity College Dublin and Stanford University, California.

Boulus, Sargon, 1944–2007
An Assyrian Iraqi, Boulus was born in Habbaniya, Iraq, and moved with his family to Kirkuk. Later, he walked across the desert to Beirut, where he lived illegally before settling in California. Fluent in Assyrian, Arabic and English, he not only wrote but also translated poetry.

Brecht, Bertolt, 1898–1956
Born in Germany, Brecht is best known for his plays and theory of 'epic theatre' in which characters represent opposing ideological arguments. He fled Nazi Germany for the US but returned to Germany after the war. His poetry, like his plays and operatic collaboration with Kurt Weill, is highly political.

Carson, Ciaran, 1948–2019
Born in Belfast, where he remained all his life, Carson published sixteen poetry collections for which he won several prizes. He also wrote about and played Irish traditional music. As Professor of English at Queen's University, Belfast, he established the Seamus Heaney Centre for Poetry.

Cohen, Andrea, 1961–
The author of eight poetry collections, Cohen is renowned for her spare and precise language. Her poetry often deals with themes of loss and memory. She directs the Blacksmith House Poetry Series in Cambridge, Massachusetts.

Crane, Stephen, 1871–1900

A war correspondent and novelist as well as a poet, Crane is best known for his American Civil War novel, *The Red Badge of Courage*, which provides a realistic rather than heroic depiction of battle. He covered the Greco-Turkish War and the Spanish-American War as a journalist, alongside his wife, Cora Taylor.

D'Aguiar, Fred, 1960–

Born in London to Guyanese parents and then raised in Guyana, D'Aguiar is a poet, novelist and playwright. His poetry often addresses issues of divided and dual identity. He moved to the US in 1994 and is currently Professor of English at the University of California, Los Angeles.

Douglas, Keith, 1920–44

Widely regarded as the best soldier-poet of the Second World War, Douglas was a tank commander in North Africa. The detached, unemotional style of his poems evokes the reality of combat. He was killed in action during the invasion of Normandy.

Ehrhart, W. D., 1948–

One of the best American poets to emerge from the Vietnam War, Ehrhart – who served with the marines - was awarded a Purple Heart for injuries he sustained fighting in Hué . He has published nine collections of poems.

Enheduana, c. 2300 BCE

A high priestess and princess who lived in Ur, in what is now Iraq, Enheduana is the earliest author whose name has been passed down in history. Her main works, written in cuneiform in the Sumerian language, were war poetry, primarily in praise of ancient deities, especially the goddess Inana.

Faiz, Faiz Ahmed, 1911–84

A celebrated and influential Urdu writer, Faiz was a journalist and member of the Communist Party as well as a poet. In 1951, he was imprisoned for four years for his alleged part in trying to overthrow the Pakistani government of the time.

Fenton, James, 1949–

Best known for war poetry inspired by his time as a journalist in Vietnam and Cambodia, Fenton has also worked as political journalist, drama critic, book reviewer and librettist. A former Oxford Professor of Poetry, he is regarded as one of the finest British poets of the age.

Holub, Miroslav, 1923–98

It wasn't until after the fall of communism that Holub's poetry was published in his home country of Czechoslovakia (now the Czech Republic). An immunologist by profession, he frequently used scientific metaphors in his poetry. Widely translated, he was much admired by other poets including Ted Hughes and Seamus Heaney.

Housman, A. E., 1859–1936

In poems that foreshadowed the First World War, Housman conjured an English pastoral idyll from which young men would soon be plucked to fight. His poetry, especially *A Shropshire Lad*, remains popular. He was already in his fifties when the war broke out so did not fight but continued as Professor of Latin at Trinity College, Cambridge.

Gershon, Karen, 1923–93

After the *Kristallnacht* attacks on Jews in 1938, Gershon and her sister were sent from Germany to Britain by *kindertransport*. She started to write poetry, mainly about the Holocaust, in English in the 1950s. After living for a while in Israel, she returned to Britain in 1973.

Kavanagh, Patrick, 1904–67
Born in County Monaghan in Ulster, Kavanagh lived for thirty-five years on his family's farm. Although his first poems about rural Irish life were published in the late 1920s, it wasn't until the mid-1950s that Kavanagh was recognised as a major Irish poet.

Kruk, Halyna, 1974–
A poet, writer of fiction and historian, Kruk has published four books of poetry and several books for children and young adults. She is Professor of Medieval Literature at the University of Lviv, Ukraine.

Kunert, Günter, 1929–2019
Born in Berlin to a Jewish mother and Catholic father, Kunert was denied a secondary education in Nazi Germany. After the war, he lived in East Germany and published his first collection of poetry in 1950. After becoming increasingly critical of the East German government, he moved to West Germany in 1979.

Makoha, Nick, 1974–
Born in Uganda, Makoha fled the country as a boy with his mother during the dictatorship of Idi Amin. He has lived in Kenya and Saudi Arabia and currently lives in London. His first collection of poetry, *Kingdom of Gravity*, was published in 2017.

Mattawa, Khaled, 1964–
Born and raised in Benghazi, Libya, Mattawa moved to the United States as a teenager in 1979. He has published four volumes of his own poetry, and numerous English translations of Arabic poetry. He is an Assistant Professor of Creative Writing at the University of Michigan.

Matur, Bejan, 1968–
A Kurdish Alevi poet born in Turkey, Matur published her first collection of poetry in 1996, followed by three others. Her poetry touches on mystical themes as well as political issues, and she is amongst the most prominent of the new female poets from the Middle East. She currently lives in London.

Mikhail, Dunya, 1965–
An Iraqi-American, Mikhail left Baghdad in 1995, eventually settling in Michigan. She has published collections of poetry in both Arabic and English. Her work touches on issues of war, exile and loss. The experience of censorship in Iraq enhanced her use of metaphor and subtext.

Milton, John, 1608–74
The epic *Paradise Lost*, written in 1667, is regarded as one of the greatest poems in the English language. Its themes include the fall of man, the temptation of Adam and Eve and the meaning of freedom. Milton was a republican, working as a civil servant under Oliver Cromwell, and was briefly gaoled in 1660 when the English monarchy was restored.

Harjo, Joy, 1951–
A performer and writer from the Muscogee (Creek) Nation, Harjo served as American Poet Laureate from 2019–2022, the first Native American to hold the post. She has produced seven music albums as well as ten volumes of poetry and is chancellor of the American Academy of Poets.

Powers, Kevin, 1980–
An American soldier-poet, Powers found his voice during the Iraq War, where he served as a machine gunner in 2004/5. His first collection of poetry, *Letter Composed During a Lull in the Fighting,*

was published in 2014. He has written two novels drawing on his experiences in Iraq.

Rossetti, Christina, 1830–94
One of the greatest poets of the Victorian age, Rossetti came from a family of poets and artists. Her most famous poem, 'Goblin Market', an allegory about the response of two sisters to temptation, remains a subject of feminist debate. She also wrote the Christmas carol 'In the Bleak Midwinter' and 'Remember', a favourite at funerals.

Sandburg, Carl, 1878–1967
A major figure in twentieth-century American literature, Sandburg won three Pulitzer Prizes – two for poetry and one for his biography of Abraham Lincoln. He also worked as a reporter in Chicago and was known as 'the singing bard', as he often performed his poems to music.

Sassoon, Siegfried, 1886–1967
Amongst the most prominent of the Great War soldier-poets, Sassoon described the horror of the trenches and satirised the generals and politicians who had no care for ordinary soldiers. After a protest against the war, he was sent to a mental hospital where he met and became friends with another poet and soldier, Wilfred Owen. Later, he wrote several thinly disguised fictional memoirs.

Saungkha, Maung, 1993–
A poet and a human rights and democracy activist, Saungkha was gaoled in 2016 for defaming Thein Sein, Myanmar's military leader, in a satirical poem. After the coup which returned the military to power in 2021, he opted for armed resistance and is currently commander of the rebel Bamar People's Liberation Army.

Seyyid, Sharmila, 1982–

A journalist, poet, writer and activist from Eravur, in Sri Lanka's Eastern Province, Seyyid has published nine books including several collections of poetry in Tamil. Exiled from Sri Lanka because of her activism, she currently lives in Nebraska.

Shelley, Percy Bysshe, 1792–1822

One of the major English Romantic poets, Shelley's turbulent life fed into his poetry which ranged from ecstasy to despair. His political and social views were regarded as radical in his day. Famed only posthumously, he was a major influence on later poets including Browning and Yeats.

Shire, Warsan, 1988–

Born in Kenya to ethnic Somali parents, Shire came to Britain as a baby. Well known for her passionate poems about the refugee experience, she collaborated with Beyoncé on her 2016 visual album *Lemonade*. Her first full-length collection of poetry, *Bless the Daughter Raised by a Voice in Her Head*, was published in 2022. She currently lives in Los Angeles.

Suhair Majaj, Lisa, 1960–

Born in the USA and raised in Jordan, the Palestinian-American poet Suhair Majaj is the author of *Geographies of Light*, which won the 2008 Del Sol Press Poetry Prize. She is also co-editor of three collections of essays on international women writers. She lives in Cyprus.

Sundaralingam, Pireeni, 1977–

Born in Sri Lanka, and brought up partly in the UK, Sundaralingham is a cognitive scientist as well as a poet. Her poems, which are often about loss of language, the erasure of identity and fear, have appeared in numerous literary journals and anthologies. She lives in San Francisco and has been appointed inaugural Poet Laureate at University College, Oxford.

Szymborska, Wisława, 1923–2012
Already well known in her native Poland, Szymborska only came to international attention when she was awarded the 1996 Nobel Prize in Literature 'for poetry that with ironic precision allows the historical and biological context to come to light in fragments of human reality'. Her poems, which have since been widely translated, often set domestic details against historical events.

Verwey, Len, 1973–
Born in Mozambique, Verwey grew up in South Africa. His first collection, *In a Language That You Know*, explores South Africa's violence, social inequality and dark history. His new book *Loving The Dying*, an exploration of the stages of a life, focusses on the tension between truth and delusion in both individuals and society.

Waterhouse, Andrew, 1958–2001
After winning the 2000 Forward Prize for his poetry collection *In*, Waterhouse was celebrated as one of Britain's most promising poets. He was also a musician and conservationist. However, he never reached his potential, as he suffered from depression and took his own life in 2001.

Xi Chuan, 1963–
One of China's most celebrated contemporary poets, essayists and literary translators, Xi Chuan is the pen name of Liu Jun. He currently teaches classical Chinese literature at the Central Academy of Fine Arts in Beijing. His poetry has been widely anthologised, and he has received numerous prizes. He has translated Ezra Pound, Luis Borges and Czesław Miłosz into Chinese.

Sources

Stories

The earliest of these stories goes back to 1986, while the most recent are from 2023/24. I wrote or broadcast versions of most at the time. None is exactly as previously written, because I have reflected on what happened or have been able to update. I would like to thank the following publications in which my writing has appeared: Channel 4 News, BBC, *New Statesman*, *Observer*, *Guardian*, *Sunday Times*, *Independent*, *Granta*, *New York Review of Books*, *Times Literary Supplement*, *Nieman Reports*, *British Journalism Review*.

Poems

Some of these poems I knew already, while others I came across online or in individual collections. Two anthologies were especially helpful. *The Hundred Years War: Modern War Poems*, ed. Neil Astley, (Bloodaxe Books, 2014) features several of the poems I have chosen. *Against Forgetting: Twentieth-Century Poetry of Witness*, ed. Carolyn Forché (W. W. Norton and Co., 1993) was also a guide. I did not choose any from *Other Men's Flowers*, selected and annotated by Lord Wavell (Jonathan Cape, 1944), but I felt he was in some ways a posthumous kindred spirit in the world of war and poetry. The foreword and afterword drew on *The Great War and Modern Memory*, by Paul Fussell (Oxford University Press, 1975), as well as Chris Hedges' *War is a Force That Gives Us Meaning* (Anchor Books, 2002) and Aminatta Forna's excellent essay, 'Who Owns Your Story? Transcending the Trauma Narrative' in the *Yale*

Review, Spring 2022. I also owe a debt of inspiration to *The Poetry Pharmacy: Tried-and-True Prescriptions for the Heart, Mind and Soul*, ed. William Sieghart (Particular Books, 2017).

Permissions

FOREWORD

Excerpt from *A German Requiem* by James Fenton from *The Memory of War and Children in Exile, Poems 1968–1983* (Penguin, 1983), reproduced by permission of Faber and Faber Ltd. Audio edition reproduced by permission of United Agents.

Excerpt from *I Belong There* by Mahmoud Darwish, translated by Carolyn Forché, from *Unfortunately, It Was Paradise: Selected Poems* (University of California Press, 2003), reproduced by permission of the University of California Press.

Excerpt from *The Place Where We are Right* by Yehuda Amichai, translated by Chana Bloch and Stephen Mitchell, from *The Selected Poetry of Yehuda Amichai* (University of California Press, 1986) reproduced by permission of the University of California Press.

To Make a Homeland by Amineh Abou Kerech from *From England – Poems from a School*, ed. Kate Clanchy (Picador 2018) reproduced by permission of the poet.

Excerpt from *Why is this Age* by Anna Akhmatova, translated by Richard McKane, from *Selected Poems* (Bloodaxe Books, 1989) reproduced by permission of Bloodaxe Books.

Excerpt from *Coriolanus* by William Shakespeare (1608) in public domain.

Excerpt from *Tell all the truth but tell it slant* by Emily Dickinson is published by Harvard University Press.

Excerpt from *Strange Meeting* by Wilfred Owen (1918), in public domain.

FIGHTERS

Here Dead Lie We by A. E. Housman (1914), in public domain.

Great Plains by Kevin Powers from *Letter Composed During a Lull in the Fighting* (Sceptre, 2014) reproduced by permission of Rogers, Coleridge & White Literary Agency and the poet.

Boy Soldier by Fred D'Aguiar from *The Rose of Toulouse* (Carcarnet, 2013) © 2013 Fred D'Aguiar, reproduced by permission of David Higham Associates.

How To Kill by Keith Douglas from *Complete Poems* (Faber, 1978), reproduced by permission of Faber.

Excerpt from *The Exaltation of Inana* by Enheduana, translated from Sumerian by Sophus Helle, from *The Complete Poems of Enheduana, the World's First Author* by Sophus Helle (Yale University Press, 2023) reproduced by permission of Sophus Helle and Yale University Press.

LOVE

Another Place by Lisa Suhair Majaj from *Geographies of Light* (Del Sol Press, 2009), reproduced by permission of the poet.

I Was Not There by Karen Gershon, from *Collected Poems* (Papermac, 1990), reproduced by permission of the estate of Karen Gershon.

Beautiful and Loving Days Gone By by Pham Ho, translated from the Vietnamese by Nguyen Ba Chung, Nguyen Quang Thieu and Bruce Weigl. Every effort has been made to contact the rightsholders at the Vietnamese Writers Association. Any further information should be sent to the publishers, Chatto & Windus, who will be pleased to make restitution.

HISTORY

COURAGE

LANDSCAPE

The Diameter of the Bomb by Yehuda Amichai (1976) translated from Hebrew by Yehuda Amichai and Ted Hughes, from *Selected Poems*, ed. Ted Hughes and Daniel Weissbort (Faber, 2000), reproduced by permission of Mrs Hana Amichai.

Grass from *The Complete Poems Of Carl Sandburg.* Copyright © 1969, 1970 by Lillian Steichen Sandburg, Trustee. Used by permission of HarperCollins Publishers.

PRISON

A Prison Evening by Faiz Ahmed Faiz (1952) translated from Urdu by Agha Shahid Ali from *The Rebel's Silhouette* (Peregrine Smith Books, 1991) reproduced by permission of the Faiz Foundation Trust and Gibbs Smith University of Massachusetts Press.

The Compulsory Reasons by Mohammed al-Maghout (2001) translated from Arabic by Noel Abdulahad, from the longer poem *Sayyaf al-Zuhur* (Flower Cutter) (Dar al-Mada, Damascus, 2001), reproduced by permission of Al Jadid Magazine.

Now the City has Fallen by Andrew Waterhouse from *In* (The Rialto, 2000), reproduced by permission of The Rialto.

Mourning Problems by Xi Chuan, translated from Chinese by Lucas Klein, from *Bloom & Other Poems*, (New Directions, 2022), © 2022 Xi Chuan, translation © 2022 Lucas Klein, reproduced by permission of New Directions Publishing Corp.

Cage by Nibha Shah, translated from Nepali by Muna Gurung (*Guernica*, 2020) reproduced by permission of N. Shah and M. Gurung.

CHILDREN

Arguments by Lisa Suhair Majaj (1998) from *Geographies of Light* (Del Sol Press, 2009), reproduced by permission of the poet.

The Child at the Window by Siegfried Sassoon (1939) from *Collected Poems 1908-1956* (Faber and Faber 1947), reproduced by permission of the Barbara Levy Literary Agency.

Eurofighter Typhoon by Fiona Benson from *Vertigo & Ghost* (Jonathan Cape, 2019), reproduced by permission of Rogers, Coleridge & White.

Your Mother's First Kiss by Warsan Shire from *Teaching My Mother How to Give Birth* (Flipped Eye, 2011), reproduced by permission of Flipped Eye.

Child of Our Time by Eavan Boland, first published in *The War Horse* (Arlen House, 1975), reprinted in *New Selected Poems* (Carcanet, 2013), reproduced by permission of Carcanet.

WARLORDS

Epitaph on a Tyrant by W. H. Auden (1939) from *Another Time* (Random House, 1940) © 1940 W. H. Auden, renewed by The Estate of W. H. Auden, reproduced by permission of Curtis Brown, Ltd.

Image by Maung Saungkha, translator unknown (*New Yorker*, 2016) reproduced by permission of the Bamar People's Liberation Army, on behalf of Maung Saungkha.

The God of War (*Der Kriegsgott*) by Bertolt Brecht, translated from German by Michael Hamburger, from *Bertolt Brecht, Werke, Große kommentierte Berliner und Frankfurter Ausgabe, Band 12: Gedichte 2*. © Bertolt-Brecht-Erben (Suhrkamp Verlag 1988), English translation reproduced by permission of Claire Hamburger.

Campaign by Len Verwey from *Otherwise Everything Goes On, Seven New Generation African Poets* (Slapering Hol Press, New York, 2014) © Len Verwey, reproduced by permission of Slapering Hol Press.

Ozymandias by Percy Bysshe Shelley (1817), in public domain.

AFTERWORD

Acknowledgements

A mysterious 'we' is frequently invoked in this book. Television journalism is a collective endeavour, so I rarely travel alone. I have worked with many colleagues over the years so am naming them here rather than in the text. Not only is Rob Hodge a great companion on the road, but he provided invaluable advice on this book and suggested the title. Soren Munk has been my essential colleague, friend and visual mentor since 9/11. Others whose work contributed to the reporting of these stories include Aleem Agha, Lizzy Amanpour, Hisham Arafat, Kerry Blackburn, Catherine Bond, Ray Bonner, Mike Borer, Frank Chicowore, Philippa Collins, Ben de Pear, Maksym Drabok, Adam Dobby, Paul Eedle, Ragnhild Ek, Jason Farringdon, Fazel Fazly, Anna-Lisa Fuglesang, Guillermo Galdos, Israel Goldvicht, Freddie Gower, Julian Hadden, Orly Halpern, Mohammad Hassan, Chris Hease, Malcolm Hicks, Stephen Hird, Josh Ho, Nick Hughes, Dani Isdale, Dareen Jubeh, Nada Kettunen, Tahir Khan, Mohammed Lagha, Nevine Mabro, Anna McIntosh-Smith, Ken McCullum, Nava Mizrahi, Hassan Morajea, Obeid Obeid, Julie O'Connor, Liam O'Hare, Sophie Orr, Jamal Osman, Ken Perry, Ray Queally, Deborah Rayner, Philomene Remy, Frances Rivers, Oumarou Saley, Bruce Shayler, Simon Stanleigh, Karim al Taee, Millicent Teasdale, Alastair Thomson, Thom Walker, Zahra Warsame, Stuart Webb and Mike Wooldridge. Apologies to anyone I have accidentally omitted. I would also like to thank the Channel 4 News Editor, Esme Wren, and the Head of Foreign News, Federico Escher, for giving me the time and space to write this book. I remain grateful to my late colleagues Sarah Corp and Graham Heslop.

In 2022, I tweeted out a poem a day while covering the war in Ukraine. Thanks to Mair Bosworth and Roger McGough who then invited me onto BBC Radio 4's 'Poetry Please', and to Kirsty Lang who encouraged me to turn the idea into a book. Others who provided support and poetry suggestions include Jon Lee Anderson, Caroline Arnold, Paul Conroy, Lyse Doucet, Lisa Dwan, Sally Fenn, Matt Frei, Zoe Goodman, Lucy Hannan, Susannah Herbert, Razia Iqbal, Christina Lamb, Allan Little, Mark Muller Stuart, Barnaby Phillips, Lemn Sissay, Margaret Ward, Jane Wellesley and Helen Wing. I am lucky to have Carrie Plitt as my agent, and Rose Tomaszewska as my editor, both of whom believed in this book, and improved it. Thanks also to Rosanna Hildyard, Rhiannon Roy and Sam Wells, and also to the late Beth Dufour, who did the painstaking work of getting permissions to reproduce the poems.

Thank you to my father, Cyril Hilsum, for putting up with me travelling to dangerous places all these years. And to Tim Lambon because of – and despite – everything.